THE ASSESSMENT OF BASIC LANGUAGE AND LEARNING SKILLS-REVISED

(The ABLLS™-R)

Scoring Instructions and IEP Development Guide

_____

The ABLLS™-R Guide

by

James W. Partington, Ph.D., BCBA

July, 2008

Version 3.1

Behavior Analysts, Inc.
P.O. Box 23695
Pleasant Hill, CA 94523-0695

www.behavioranalysts.com

THE ASSESSMENT OF BASIC LANGUAGE AND LEARNING SKILLS (THE ABLLS™-R): SCORING INSTRUCTIONS AND IEP DEVELOPMENT GUIDE

July, 2008
Version 3.1

Partington, James W.

The ABLLS™-R is an assessment tool based on a criterion-referenced set of skills that can demonstrate a student's current repertoire and provides for the tracking of its progressive development. However, this assessment does not determine or prioritize whether any of these skills may be important for any particular student's development or suggest that it is necessary for all of them to be included. Furthermore, it should not be viewed that the attainment of all the skills by a child with a developmental disability would result in "normal development or functioning." It is not within the scope of this instrument to determine the appropriateness of any educational goals and objectives, nor the priority of a child's needs. Rather, it is recommended that users confer with a trained and experienced professional to evaluate an individual's need and to determine appropriate educational priorities and programming decisions.

The ABLLS™-R is an update to The Assessment of Basic Language and Learning Skills (The ABLLS) that was published in 1998. The revisions to the original version were made with input from many professionals in the fields of education, behavior analysis, and speech and language pathology.

ISBN: 0-9745151-5-9

Publisher: Behavior Analysts, Inc.
              Attn: James W. Partington, Ph.D.
              P.O. Box 23695
              Pleasant Hill, CA 94523-0695

              www.behavioranalysts.com
              (925) 210-9378
              FAX (925) 210-0436

Dedication

In loving memory of my parents, William C. Partington and Sonja M. (Polson) Partington who constantly modeled concern for others, demonstrated a ready willingness to extend themselves to help others in times of need, and through their smiles, shared with all, the joy of living.

JWP

Acknowledgments

Skinner's (1957) analysis of verbal behavior serves as the conceptual basis for the current language-based, skills assessment. The first published program that used Skinner's analysis of verbal behavior for language assessment was the Parsons Language Sample (Spradlin, 1963). Dr. Spradlin was a pioneer in the use of Skinner's analysis of verbal behavior for individuals with developmental disabilities, and has inspired a number of follow-up projects on behavioral language assessment (e.g., Sloane & MacAuley, 1968; Sundberg, 1983; Sundberg, Ray, Braam, Stafford, Rueber, & Braam, 1980). Many elements of the current assessment are derived from Spradlin's early work, as well as these subsequent projects.

This current version of The ABLLS™-R has been the result of many years of work and included input from a variety of sources. As with most projects of this scope, there are numerous individuals who have contributed in various ways to the development of the final product. There have been numerous substantive contributions from colleagues and the staff at Behavior Analysts, Inc. In particular, the author wishes to acknowledge the input from Cathleen Bailey, Monica Berryhill, Laurie Bochner, CCC-SLP, Dr. Sharon Bradley-Johnson, Deb Brown, Autumn Burnside, Schelley Conklin, Gwen Dwiggins, Katie Endicott, Michelle Gansen-Hedegaard, David Garcia, Nancy Hanebury, Jamie Hughes, Nikki Judd, Carmen Martin, Kat Mulcahy, Dr. Pamela Osnes, Danielle Owens, Dr. Mary Ann Powers, Cathy Santopadre, Denise Senick-Pirri, CCC-SLP, Michelle Sullivan, Dr. Mark Sundberg, Becky Watson, and Rob Willis. Additionally, there have been numerous individuals who have given encouragement to see the product through to completion. The author is particularly grateful to our mentors, Dr. Jack Michael and Dr. Jon Bailey, and friends, Dr. Gerald Shook, Sharon Brenneise, Gary and Judy Collins, Lorie Schultz, Barbara Young, and Ed Santopadre, for their encouragement along the way. The author is also appreciative of the administrative support provided to us by Fred and Julie Madriaga, Roz Kuritz, Carol Tallman, and Laurie Winkler who helped us find time to get the work done.

Most importantly, I would like to acknowledge my family for enduring our countless hours of work on this project. I owe a great deal to my wife, Terry Partington, and my children, Scott and Sonja Partington, for their patience, support, and continuous examples of verbal behavior.

Of course, this work would be meaningless if it were not for the parents and children served by devoted professionals and the staff who work with the children. Thanks to all the children who have taught us so much.

Table of Contents

1

Introduction to The ABLLS™-R

The Assessment of Basic Language and Learning Skills-Revised (The ABLLS™-R) is an assessment, curriculum guide, and skills tracking system for children with language delays. *The ABLLS™-R* contains a task analysis of many of the skills necessary to communicate successfully and to learn from everyday experiences. The revised version is an update of an earlier version of The ABLLS (Partington & Sundberg, 1998) and includes many new items that help to identify specific skill strengths and weaknesses. A thorough description of the changes in the assessment can be found in Appendix 1).

The ABLLS™-R is comprised of two separate documents: *The ABLLS™-R Protocol* that is used to record scores for each child, and *The ABLLS™-R Scoring Instructions and IEP Development Guide (The ABLLS™-R Guide)*. *The ABLLS™-R Protocol* provides both parents and professionals with criterion-referenced information regarding a child's current skills that can serve as a basis for the selection of educational objectives. *The ABLLS™-R Protocol* also includes a set of grids that comprise a skills tracking system that make it possible to observe and document the child's progress in the acquisition of critical skills, and to identify skill areas that remain in need of further development.

The current book, *The ABLLS™-R Guide,* serves two purposes. First, it provides instructions for scoring *The ABLLS™-R Protocol* and for completing the skills tracking grids for an individual student. Second, it provides strategies to assist parents, educators and other professionals to use the information obtained from the completed assessment protocol to develop an effective Individualized Education Program (IEP) for the child.

Although *The ABLLS™-R Protocol* provides an extensive list of skills, it does not include a method to readily determine the educational priorities that should be addressed for an individual child and does not include the specific steps necessary to teach those skills. The selection of learning tasks and specific teaching methods must be carefully considered when developing educational programs. *The ABLLS™-R Guide* provides strategies for analyzing *The ABLLS™-R* scores to help determine educational priorities, and help with the selection of appropriate educational objectives for an individual child.

The ABLLS™-R Protocol and *The ABLLS™-R Guide* are two books in a series of publications from Behavior Analysts, Inc., that can help parents and educators with the process of identifying specific skills that should be the focus of intervention with a given child with language delays. The companion book, *Teaching Language to Children With Autism or Other Developmental Disabilities* (Sundberg & Partington, 1998) provides detailed descriptions about how to teach those critical skills. A fourth publication, *A Collection of Reprints on Verbal Behavior* (Sundberg & Michael, 1998) contains conceptual and empirical research articles regarding the behavioral approach to language.

Purpose

The purpose of *The ABLLS™-R* is to identify those language and other critical skills that are in need of intervention in order for a child to become more capable of learning from his everyday experiences. These skills are delineated in the Basic Learner Skills section of *The ABLLS™-R Protocol*. A secondary purpose is to provide a method for identifying a child's specific skills in a variety of other important areas including academic, self-help, and motor skills. Finally, *The ABLLS™-R Protocol* provides a curriculum guide for an educational program for a child with language delays and provides a method for visually displaying the acquisition of new skills on the tracking system.

Rationale

Parents and educators who live and work with a child with language delays know there are a variety of skills that each child must acquire. The acquisition of what to others may seem to be a minor skill is often viewed as a major "breakthrough" for those involved in the child's intervention. However, those involved realize the amount of time and the sophistication of the teaching methodology is greatly magnified compared to what is required for a typically-developing child to achieve a similar skill.

It is important for parents and educators to know what a child can and cannot do in order to know which skills need to be the focus of current instruction. Teaching a few critical skills may result in the faster acquisition of a larger set of skills without the need for sophisticated teaching and elaborate motivational conditions. Educational activities for children with language delays should focus on teaching the child those skills that will result in a child being able to learn from non-structured daily activities. Most children can benefit from effective teaching strategies implemented by a competent teacher. However, it is important that the child develop a set of generalized learning skills that allows him to learn many skills without the benefit of a highly-trained instructor. Therefore, a criterion-referenced assessment of language and other critical learning skills can serve as a basis for identifying a child's current skills. It can also serve as a guide for selecting new skills to develop such that the child will "learn to learn" without highly-specialized instruction.

Special Features

Although there are numerous assessments that address many of the areas covered by this assessment, this document is unique in several respects. *The ABLLS™-R Protocol* has been designed to assess a variety of language skills. It has also been designed to account for a child's motivation to respond, his ability to attend to a variety of environmental stimuli (verbal and nonverbal), his ability to generalize skills, and his tendency to spontaneously use those skills. These features will be described in more detail.

Language

The most significant feature of *The ABLLS™-R* is that it is an assessment based on the behavioral analysis of language as presented by Dr. B. F. Skinner in his book *Verbal Behavior* (1957). Skinner's analysis of language has proven to be extremely valuable in helping to identify the contexts in which individuals use language, and the importance of teaching language under all of these different environmental contexts.

Skinner's analysis of language is a functional analysis in that it primarily focuses on the different environmental (i.e., pragmatic) conditions in which language occurs. As a result of this approach, Skinner has identified several different types of expressive language. These different types of expressive language are typically combined in other language assessments, and thus, may conceal specific language deficits. Skinner's analysis has demonstrated to be an important tool for both identifying the specific language deficits experienced by many children with autism, as well as point to areas most in need of intervention.

Motivation

Many of the assessment items in *The ABLLS™-R* were incorporated to provide an analysis of the motivational conditions that may affect a child. It is often found that certain skills will only be demonstrated when either naturally–occurring motivational situations are captured or when certain motivational situations are contrived. Therefore, many of the task items are designed to help identify the child's skills under a variety of motivational conditions. Additionally, the child's ability to be reinforced by praise and other socially oriented types of reinforcers is reviewed.

Complex Stimuli

In order to learn from ongoing experiences, individuals need to be able to attend to all of the critical stimuli present. *The ABLLS™-R* assesses the child's ability to attend to a variety of combined stimuli. Many children with language delays, especially children with autism, have difficulty attending to certain combinations of stimuli (e.g., a task involving a combination of both verbal and visual stimuli). Several of the items in *The ABLLS™-R* assess this ability because so many elements of language in the natural environment involve complex stimulus conditions.

Generalization

The ABLLS™-R assesses a child's ability to generalize language skills to new situations. Most children can learn specific skills;

however, those skills may not be helpful to a child unless he can use those skills in a variety of situations. It is important that the language skills occur when different materials, are presented by different people, at different times, in different social settings, and in different verbal contexts.

Spontaneity

The *ABLLS™-R* assesses a child's ability to use language skills without prompts from others. A child's spontaneous use of language is a very important marker in language acquisition, and its absence needs to be identified and appropriately addressed in the intervention program.

Fluency

One of the major research areas with regard to skill development has been related to the concern that students often acquire basic skills but lack the ability to quickly use them when they are required in a variety of contexts (e.g., learning more complex skills that require the basic skills, using the skills during everyday activities). Therefore, the revised version of the ABLLS™-R Protocol includes scoring criteria to help ensure that children are capable of using their acquired skills in a fluent manner.

Joint Attention

Another area of considerable research has been related to the ability of children to share attention with others to items and events that occur in the presence of both individuals. This ability to see that others are also observing a similar item or event is a skill that is critical for the development of more advanced social interactions. As a result, several new items have been added to the current version to help with the tracking and development of this important skill area.

Learner Readiness

One of the major factors that influences a student's ability to acquire new skills is his willingness to follow the directions from those who are attempting to teach him. Therefore, the task of the instructor is considerably easier when the student is able to follow a sequence of directions for intermittent social reinforcers than when the student requires frequent powerful reinforcers in order to follow very simple directions. The current version of the ABLLS™-R has incorporated several new items to measure the student's ability to work both with a variety of individuals and to do so while attending to reinforcing feedback of a social nature.

Additionally, many educational tasks require the presentation of materials in a display that can best be presented on a table. Therefore, it is critical that children learn a variety of skills related to participation with an instructor who has placed the material in front of the student. Specifically, the child needs to be able to focus on the materials, attend to the instructions being provided to him and then follow through with the requested actions in a timely manner.

Social Skills Development

The development of effective social interaction skills has been an area of concern for many individuals with developmental disabilities. The recent focus of specific interventions to develop these skills has helped with the identification of many of the subtle skills that are needed by individuals to be able to interact with and learn from their peers. Many of these skills have been added to the revised version of the ABLLS™-R.

Imitation

The importance of having a well-developed imitative repertoire has been recognized by parents and professionals as critical to development of a wide variety of language, self-help, motor, academic and social skills. The updated version of the ABLLS™-R Protocol has incorporated many new skill items that help to extend the parent's and professional's ability to determine the extent of a child's ability to attend to the subtle features of the actions of others and to the ability to replicate those actions. Many of the new skills have been included to ensure both greater amount of time attending to the behaviors being modeled by others and to the ability to recall those actions following the demonstrated actions.

Skills Tracking System

The ABLLS™-R provides the user with not only the initial assessment of skills, but also allows for reviews and updates of a child's progress. The initial assessment may be conducted informally over a period of several weeks. After the initial assessment is completed, the results of the assessment can be displayed on the skills tracking system's display grids that portray the level at which a child is performing specific skills. In addition, skill deficits are clearly identified, thus providing valuable information for developing intervention targets.

As a child's assessment is updated, it is possible to display the gains observed in the various skill areas by filling in additional boxes. This updating process provides a great source of reinforcement for parents and educators as they see that critical skills are being acquired.

Limitations

Although there are many skills covered in The ABLLS™-R Protocol, it is not considered to be an exhaustive list of skills and does not identify all of the steps in the teaching process that may be necessary to teach the skills. An attempt has been made to arrange the items in an approximate developmental sequence. The sequence of skills delineated in The ABLLS™-R has been modified based upon its use with children with language delays (mainly with a diagnosis of Autism Spectrum Disorder) and from data regarding the performance of several typically developing young children of a similar age (Partington, Dwiggins & Osnes, in preparation). Task items within each section have been arranged in an order such that the lowest numbered items are generally acquired prior to those that follow. However, since many individuals with language delays acquire skills out of the typical developmental sequence, the need for such ordering is not considered to be of primary importance.

The ABLLS™-R is not designed to provide age norms, nor is it designed to compare the learner's skills to those of a defined peer group. It is designed to serve as a criterion-referenced skills assessment to be used to identify where to begin language intervention and what potential language objectives might be appropriate for a child's Individual Education Plan (IEP). After a period of time, the assessment can be updated to document a child's acquisition of skills and allow for a re-analysis of the educational priorities and strategies.

Many children with language delays engage in disruptive or interfering behaviors that often make it difficult to teach them skills. Many, if not most of these behaviors result in the child either avoiding and/or escaping from tasks, or in the attainment of attention from others. These behaviors are often a result of the teaching methodology used with the child and can be reduced or eliminated by careful adjustment of the teaching strategies. Because disruptive and inappropriate behaviors are often very complex in nature, it is not possible to include methods for conducting a functional analysis of these problems in this document. There are several books that provide information that provide assistance with the analysis of these types of behaviors (e.g., Cooper, Heron & Heward, 1987; Foxx, 1982; Martin & Pear, 2002).

Scoring The ABLLS™-R

Who Can Complete The Assessment

The ABLLS™-R Protocol can be completed by a parent, educator, behavior analyst, psychologist, speech and language therapist, or other professional (or a combination of these individuals) who has thoroughly studied the *Protocol* and has frequent and direct contact with the student. It is recommended that the person who is responsible for developing and/or monitoring the educational program for a particular individual collect the information, and that the individual or team of individuals who completes this assessment be knowledgeable of the process of conducting assessments and in interpretation of the assessment results.

It should be noted that determining the skills of a student is only one step in the development of a program to increase a student's skills; knowledge about planning both what and how to teach is the next step and requires input from individuals who have been trained in the areas of program development and implementation. The companion book, *Teaching Language to Children with Autism or Other Developmental Disabilities* (Sundberg & Partington, 1998) provides additional information regarding assessment procedures and interpretation of assessment information that has a high degree of correspondence with the information obtained from *The ABLLS™-R* and also provides considerable information about procedures to teach many important language skills.

Sources of Information

Information to complete *The ABLLS™-R* is obtained from three sources. The majority of the information will be obtained from parents, educators, and others who regularly interact with the child. It is desirable to seek information from several individuals who regularly interact with the child to get the clearest picture of the child's abilities and how he typically uses those skills. The second source of information will come from observation of the child in particular situations. It is important to not only determine the levels of a child's skills, but to also have an understanding of how the child typically uses those skills. As such, it would not be appropriate for information to be gathered about a student without actually having the opportunity to watch the child. The third source of information will be obtained from the formal presentation of tasks to the child to determine the child's competence with specific skills.

Overview of the Scoring Format

The ABLLS™-R has a consistent format for each item. Specifically, each item has a row of columns that includes a task number, range of scores, task name, task objective, question to ask about the child's skill, examples of responses (as required for clarification), scoring criteria, and notes section.

The Notes Section

The notes section is provided to make brief notations regarding particular issues related to a child's performance. The information about specific issues related to the performance of a skill can be particularly helpful in determining skills to be developed or further generalized. For example, it is not uncommon for a parent to note that a child eats his food neatly, and for his caregiver to indicate that he does not keep his area clean while eating. Both may be accurate, and an investigation may need to be made to understand the differences in how the child is fed in both situations and to ensure that eating neatly is reinforced in all locations. Additionally, if the child is demonstrating a skill but only in limited circumstances, it may be important to note those circumstances such that an effort can be made to get the skill to occur under other situations.

Notations that refer the assessor to the appendices, where detailed information on a particular task may be recorded and notes regarding some issues related to skill development are found in this section. Additionally, notation has also been made so that users of the previous version of the *ABLLS™ Protocol* can quickly see if an item has been added (marked as "New"), or has been "Modified."

The Score Column

There are four rows of numbers in the scoring column for each task item. The numbers in the "Score" column correspond with the possible scores in the "Criteria" column. The scores in the "Score" column range from zero to the highest score in the "Criteria" column (i.e., either 1, 2, or 4). A score of zero (on the far left of the column) indicates that the child does not meet the lowest criterion specified for that task item as defined in the "Criteria" column. The number on the far right of the column is the highest score possible for that task. Thus, depending upon the particular task, the scoring column will have four rows with the numbers 0 1; 0 1 2; or 0 1 2 3 4. The top row of scores for each item is for the initial skills assessment. The remaining three rows are available for three updates of *The ABLLS™-R Protocol*.

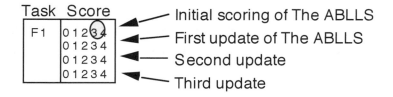

How to Score Individual Items

The process of scoring *The ABLLS™-R Protocol* involves reviewing each task and assigning a score to the item. Scores are assigned by circling the number that represents the level of performance as specified in the CRITERIA column.

TASK	SCORE	TASK NAME	TASK OBJECTIVE	QUESTION	CRITERIA	NOTES
G 4	0 1 2 3 4 0 1 2 3 4 0 1 2 3 4 0 1 2 3 4	Labels **pictures** of common items	The student will label at least 100 pictures of items which are commonly found in his environment.	If you ask "What is that?" when shown a picture of a common item, will the student identify the item?	4= 100 or more labels of pictures of items and can identify several different examples (including novel examples) of most of those items, 3= 50 labels of at least one example of the item, 2= 10 labels, 1= 5 labels	See Appendix 3: Receptive and Label List

When completing *The ABLLS™-R Protocol*, it is important to ensure that individuals who provide information regarding the child's skill level actually know the child's true skill level, rather than guess as to the actual level. If the exact level of performance on a task is not known, the exact skill level can be determined through direct observation of the child's skills or through more formal assessment.

It is very important that the responses given to *The ABLLS™-R* questions be provided based upon both the child's knowledge and his typical use of the skill. Specifically, it is important not to overestimate the child's skills by indicating emerging skills, or those skills that the learner has demonstrated in the past, but does not currently exhibit. The information requested is **what the child typically does or can do when required**, not what he is beginning to do, or what he has done in the past (e.g., several months or years ago). If the child has clearly and consistently demonstrated the skill on numerous occasions but is not demonstrating the skill at the moment (possibly due to motivational issues), the student should be given credit for what individuals who work with him know he can do under the correct motivational situation.

In general, it is better to underestimate a child's skill levels than to overestimate the level of performance because scores that do not meet the highest criterion level will be more likely to be reviewed for consideration of intervention. Therefore, if the child's skills are weak, he will benefit from the teaching interventions. However, if the scores are overestimated, the child may not develop those critical skills; and furthermore, the child may be given educational tasks which are too difficult for him that may contribute to the occurrence of disruptive behaviors.

When the child's current level of performance on a particular task is clearly known, the appropriate score should be given for that task. It is important to identify the highest score for which the child actually meets the specified criteria for each item. If a child has more skill than is required for a particular score (e.g., a score of "3"), but does not fully meet the criteria for the next score (e.g., a score of "4"), then the lower score should be given for that task.

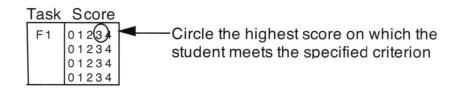

For all tasks that a child is unable to do, or cannot meet the criterion for the lowest possible score for that task, that task should be scored "zero." Also, if a child has skill deficits that prevent him from being able to participate in a particular activity (e.g., group instruction) that is assessed by an item, that item should be scored "zero."

Children have skills that may only be observed under specific conditions. For example, when shown a picture of a truck and asked, "What is this?" the child might merely respond, "a truck." However, when shown the same picture and asked to "tell me about this picture," the child may be able to identify it as "a big blue garbage truck." Thus, the child should be acknowledged for being able to combine adjectives with nouns, even though this skill is only observed to occur under certain conditions. However, if the child could not provide such a description without specific prompts to get each part of the response (e.g., What color is the truck? What do people put in the truck? Is it a big or little truck?), he should not be given credit for having the skill of combining adjectives with nouns. Thus, although the child has the ability to label specific attributes, he does not have the ability to label items using those adjectives.

There are two items that may not be applicable to all children. Task H3 is not applicable for children who use speech to communicate and have never used American Sign Language (ASL), and ASL is clearly not appropriate as a method of communication. Additionally, Task X5 is a toileting skill that is only applicable to females. When either of these two task items is not applicable for a child, "NA" should be circled in the score box for that item.

How to Do the Initial Scoring of the Assessment

It is expected that the initial assessment of skills will be completed in several steps. The first step is to review the items of the assessment with respect to what is clearly known about the child. Specifically, the goal is to determine both those skills for which the child meets the criterion for the highest score for the item (e.g., a score of 4), and those items for which the child does not meet any of the specified criteria (e.g., a score of 0). The score sections for those task items for which the child's level of performance is unknown should be left blank, as they will be filled in during the next step of the process. However, during this first step of the assessment when the exact level of the skill is unknown, it is often beneficial to define the range of scores that may include the child's skill level (e.g., the score is either a 2 or a 3, but is definitely not a 0 nor a 4).

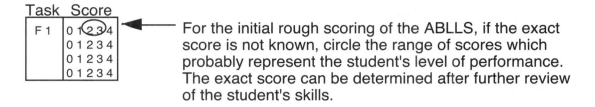

Task Score

For the initial rough scoring of the ABLLS, if the exact score is not known, circle the range of scores which probably represent the student's level of performance. The exact score can be determined after further review of the student's skills.

When gathering information regarding a student's skills, it is important that the student actually be observed in a variety of activities and settings while interacting with several instructors and peers. Attempting to gather the information without seeing the student does not allow one to get an accurate view of how the child is using his skills. It is also beneficial to observe the child on more than one day in order to view the stability of the student's performance.

When discussing the student's specific skills, it is beneficial to ask for the same information from several people who frequently interact with the child when he may be using the skills (e.g., parents, teacher, speech and language pathologist). It helps identify skills that the person may be able to teach during their interactions with the student and helps to ensure the accuracy of the information about the student's skills.

Whenever there is a discrepancy between reports about a particular skill, it is often helpful to note that information in the "Notes" section of the Protocol, and to then further investigate the reasons for the discrepancy. In some cases, one of the informants may not have understood the specifics of the task, or the person may have assumed that the student had the skill because they did not realize that they were unintentionally prompting the child to complete the task, or otherwise arranged the task such that the child could or could not do the task. In other cases there may be situations in which the child will cooperate with one individual to a higher degree than with another person because of the structure of the interactions or due to the student's history of reinforcement for cooperation with the individuals. When observing the child, it may be possible to determine the variations in the task or motivation of the child that may be responsible for the variation in performance.

Once those items that the child has mastered and those items that the child is clearly unable to do have been identified, the second step is to more precisely determine the child's abilities for the remainder of the skills. This second step may involve both observations and formal assessment of the child's skills.

Special Scoring Notes

Classroom and Group Skills Sections

Some young children are not participating in classroom or group activities. Because they are not participating in such situations, their scores should be marked as not occurring (i.e., zero). The fact that they are not in a classroom or group situation should be noted in the "Note" section. When they do enter a classroom or group, the scores can be updated during the next update process.

Receptive Skills Section

It should be noted that some of the initial levels of the early level receptive skills gives credit to a student for responding receptively (i.e., following a direction) when in actuality, the student may be given other prompts in order to complete the specified task. Credit is given at this early stage because it is a step in the direction of being able to complete these tasks without prompts. For example, in Receptive Skills item C2 "Follow instructions to do an enjoyable action in context," the criterion for a score of "1" specifies being able to do 3 or more activities with only partial physical prompts. To receive the highest score for this task item (i.e., a score of "4"), the student must be able to do at least 3 activities without prompts.

Requesting Skills Section

Some of the first few items in the Requesting sequence (i.e., F2 – F 6) are all similar skills, but vary in terms of the context in which the request is made. The earlier skills that allow the use of prompts and the presence of the item being requested were included as steps toward the development of the latter skill where these prompts and presence of the item is not required. At the highest criterion of the skill (i.e., F6 score of 4) the student must be able to request 10 or more specific items or activities when the items or items associated with the activities are not present. Therefore, if the student can request items when the item is not present and when no other prompts are provided, the student should receive credit for the highest level of F2-F5).

Stability of Scores

It appears that when care is taken to get an adequate sample of the student's skill levels, and the scores for the skills are scored conservatively (i.e., ensure that the skill is a strong skill, scoring at a lower level if not absolutely certain that the skill is a well-established skill) and that the skills that have been taught to the student are ones that will be regularly used in their daily activities, the scores of the skills usually do not decrease. The importance of striving to teach skills that are useful for the child in their daily activities cannot be overstated. Learned skills can easily be forgotten if there are not opportunities to consistently use them. Hopefully, with the implementation of effective teaching strategies, the student's skills will continue to improve.

One of the areas where skills may appear to vary from one assessment to an update of the assessment is in the Cooperation and Reinforcer Effectiveness Section. It should be noted that a student's willingness to cooperate with individuals is constantly changing as the value of the potential reinforcer changes and as the amount of effort required to earn that reinforcer changes. Similarly, a student's willingness to work with any individual is also a function of the history of reinforcement associated with that person. If the student has established a strong working relationship with a particular instructor, the student may not work as well with other individuals who have not established a strong reinforcing relationship with the student.

However, there are certain other exceptions to observed decreases in skill levels. The exceptions usually include inaccurate initial scoring of the items or a fluctuation in the ability of individuals to motivate the child (especially in the scores of the Cooperation and Reinforcer Effectiveness section). When it is consistently difficult to motivate a child to engage in activities, it may be difficult to get a very accurate determination of the student's actual skills. Whenever this situation is apparent, it is most important to develop the student's cooperation (i.e., establish instructional control) such that the skill levels can be more accurately determined.

Lastly, and unfortunately, in an extremely small group of students, there has been a clear and dramatic regression in skills that has been associated with the onset of significant seizure activity. Under this unfortunate circumstance, it is probably best to begin a new assessment protocol.

Transfer to Tracking Grids On the Skills Tracking System

Once the scores for the initial assessment items have been determined, it is then necessary to transfer the scores to the corresponding grid boxes on the skills tracking system sheets. The score for each item specifies the number of boxes to be filled with a felt-tipped marker on the line corresponding to the task number on the assessment protocol. The range of scores for most items is from zero ("can't do the task") to four (mastery), but some items are scored from zero to two (mastery), and other items are scored either zero or one (mastery). Those items scored as "NA" on *The ABLLS™-R Protocol* scoring sheets (H3 & X5) should be marked with diagonal lines (////////) in the corresponding skill area on the skills tracking system sheets.

There is an open circle to the left of each task number (e.g., B8) listed on the summary grid sheets. During the initial completion of the assessment, the circle is to be filled in for those items on which the child received a score of zero. The filled circle indicates that the item was reviewed, but that the child could not do that task during the initial assessment (i.e., a score of zero).

Because the assessment may be completed over a period of several days or weeks, it is not necessary to specify an exact date of the assessment. The assessment does not compare the child's scores to the statistical scores for children of a specific age, so it is not necessary to calculate the child's exact age (i.e., years, months). It is sufficient to know the approximate date or even the month and year that the assessment was completed.

Development of An Educational Plan

After the initial assessment (or update) of *The ABLLS™-R Protocol* is completed and the skills tracking system grids have been filled in, it is possible for the child's clinical team (i.e., parents, teachers, behavior analysts, psychologists, speech therapists, and others involved with the child) to design and implement an educational plan to address the issues deemed to be the most critical for the child. It is not possible to provide a description of how to develop a specific educational plan for every potential combination of skills and skill deficits. However, information presented in subsequent chapters of this book provide strategies for determining educational priorities and for developing an effective IEP. It is recommended that the clinical team carefully consider emphasizing the development of skills included in the Basic Learner Skills section of *The ABLLS™-R* (i.e., sections A through K). The skills included in this section of *The ABLLS™-R* are extremely valuable in helping the child become able to learn without highly individualized and specialized instruction.

Because of the unique learning histories of students with developmental delays, it is not possible to determine an exact level of task difficulty and develop an exact sequence of skill acquisition for any skill repertoire area. It must be remembered that the skills in each sequence are related to skills in other repertoires areas; a skill acquired in one area (e.g., receptive language) may make it possible to acquire a skill in a different area (e.g., labeling or intraverbal). The selection of skills to be taught to a student must be done on an individual basis. As such, it is important for individuals who are developing educational programs for specific students to select skills to be taught based upon the student's readiness to learn each skill, rather than merely selecting a skill because it is a lower task item than some items that have been acquired by the student, or because it is the next item in the sequence that has not yet been acquired.

The companion book, *Teaching Language to Children with Autism or Other Developmental Disabilities* (Sundberg & Partington, 1998) provides useful information regarding interpretation of assessment information similar to the information obtained from *The ABLLS™-R Protocol*. It provides specific teaching procedures that can be used to teach those skills that are determined to be currently in need of development.

Updating the Assessment

After the completion of the initial scoring of *The ABLLS™-R Protocol*, the assessment provides the opportunity for three updates of the child's skills. Updating of *The ABLLS™-R Protocol* should be conducted at least yearly, especially immediately prior to the development of a child's IEP objectives (e.g., one month prior to the next IEP in which new learning objectives will be required). The update can be used to identify progress that has occurred both as a result of specific training, and as a result of learning that occurred without specialized instruction. For a child who is rapidly acquiring the skills measured by *The ABLLS™-R Protocol*, it may be helpful to complete an update approximately every four to six months. It is not recommended that *The ABLLS™-R* be updated whenever a child meets the next criterion level for each skill. It is more important to focus on the overall skill development as opposed to the moment-to-moment acquisition.

The updating process is considerably easier than the initial assessment in that only changes observed in the skills are noted on the protocol and the summary grid. Because an extensive review of skills was conducted during the initial assessment, there is no need to formally assess progress by reintroducing the tasks during an update review. The information for the update can be obtained by informal observation of the child and from information provided by teachers, parents, and others who frequently interact with the child.

The updating process involves scanning the score column for each item. There are four rows of numbers in the scoring column that are used for conducting the initial scoring and three updates of *The ABLLS™-R Protocol*. All items that have the highest score circled (i.e., the number on the right side of the score column) during either the initial assessment or during a previous update can usually be skipped, because the child has met the maximum criterion for that task. There is no need to repeatedly circle the highest score once the maximum score has been attained. Information about the child's improvement in a skill is recorded by circling the new (higher) score in the appropriate row of numbers in the score column. If the child has made no progress in a particular skill, the same number that was circled on the previous review should be circled on the row of scores for the current update. By circling those scores that remain unchanged, it is possible to assume that the score for that task has been reviewed and is still in need of development.

Although the scores for skills usually increase or remain the same for each of the tasks, it is possible for a child to actually receive a lower score on a task item than was obtained during a previous assessment. As mentioned earlier, a reduction in the score for a task is often an indication of an inaccurate assessment (overestimation the child's skills) of that particular skill during a previous assessment, but it can also be indicative of an actual decrease in the skill level (e.g., forgot the skill because it was not used).

Transfer Update Data to Grids

When filling in the grid boxes of the skills tracking system during the updating process, it is important to use a marker of a different color than that used following the initial assessment or during previous updates. The different colors allow for easy identification of progress observed during the intervention periods. Because the circles to the left of each task have been filled in during the initial assessment, indicating that the student did not meet the lowest criterion for those items, the circles should not be changed in the updating process. Instead, any increase in the skill level should now be indicated in the boxes on the grid for that skill.

Sample ABLLS scores

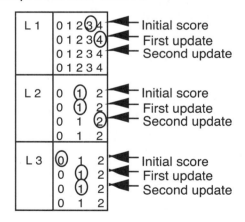

Corresponding filled-in grids on
the Skills Tracking System

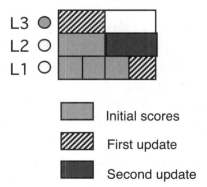

Determining Educational Priorities

The Goal: Learning to learn

The parent or teacher of a child with language delays is often easily able to identify language deficits by comparing the child to typical children of the same age. For example, a typical five-year-old child is able to readily ask for a variety of items and activities, can name and receptively identify thousands of items and activities, knows colors, numbers, letters, and is able to learn a variety of new concepts with relatively little effort. Thus, for the child of that age who has only a limited vocabulary, there are clearly many skills that the child could develop to reduce the discrepancy in skill levels from his peers (Partington, Dwiggins, & Osnes, in preparation).

Unfortunately, merely identifying deficits does not often result in effective educational practices. A skill that may appear at first glance to be a relatively simple task (e.g., follow instructions to touch a specific item, or receptively identify colors) may prove to be difficult for a child to learn, and may result in frustration for the parent or teacher.

For the child with autism or other developmental disabilities, it is often critical that those who attempt to teach him are well trained in behavioral teaching methodologies and have a well-sequenced curriculum that can be individualized to meet the specific needs of a child. The combination of effective teaching practices and an appropriate curriculum can help to maintain a child's motivation during the instructional activities.

Although one could identify all the skills that a child needs to learn, and then begin to teach each of those specific skills, this approach may not be practical. A more efficient strategy may be to teach the child skills that will allow him to learn additional skills without the need for highly-specialized instruction. Therefore, a curriculum should emphasize teaching a child a set of basic learner skills such that he will "learn to learn."

The Basic Learner Skills

The Basic Learner Skills section of *The ABLLS™-R Protocol* provides a basis for a curriculum that emphasizes skills that are important for being able to "learn to learn." Therefore, the majority of instructional time should be devoted to the development of these critical skills. While other skills may also be taught concurrently with these skills (e.g., self-help and motor skills), it is often beneficial to postpone certain tasks (e.g., traditional academic skills) until progress has been made on the basic learner skills (unless the child shows a high degree of interest in learning those skills).

The Basic Learner Skills section is comprised of 15 important skill areas that appear to be critical in order to learn from everyday experiences. These skill areas include the child's cooperation with learning activities, specific receptive and expressive language skills, imitation, social interaction, appropriate play, participation in group instruction, following classroom routines, and generalization of acquired skills. This section of the *ABLLS™-R Protocol* includes 382 skill items and represents 70 percent of the total number of items included in the assessment.

In the process of developing the original task analysis of the basic learner skills (The ABLLS, 1998), a review of the skills demonstrated by typically-developing, kindergarten-age children was conducted. The review was important for two reasons. First, typically-developing children do not require highly-specialized instruction when they enter kindergarten. With careful presentation of topics in a group instructional format, these children can quickly acquire a wide variety of academic and social skills. Thus, their demonstration of these skills tends to provide a measure of validity for the items selected for this section. Secondly, because most (but not all) of the skills contained in Basic Learner Skills section are ones that most typically-developing children would have acquired by the end of kindergarten (Partington, Dwiggins, & Osnes, in preparation). These skills represent a reasonable, age-based target for young children who are in early intervention programs, while also continuing to provide important educational goals for older learners. It is important to consider that if an older learner has not acquired some of these basic skills, the development of these skills could help the individual gain access to a wider range of options for involvement in community activities.

Development of All Basic Skills

Even though there are many skills included in each of the 15 areas of the Basic Learner Skills Section, it is important that an emphasis be placed on developing skills in each of the skill areas rather than over-emphasizing the development of one or two of those areas. It is at least as important to develop skills in all of the areas as it is to continue developing existing strengths within an area. Although it can often be very exciting to watch a child progress from being able to receptively identify and label 30 items to being able to identify 200 items, it is at least equally and probably more important that the child learn to request some of those items and talk about some of those items (i.e., intraverbals). It is important to remember that teaching a particular skill most often results in the child developing several important related skills.

Teaching Skills Across Repertoire Areas

When teaching a specific task to a student, it is important to remember that the teaching activity can facilitate the development of several skill areas. For example, when teaching a child to request an item (e.g., raisin) the instructor is able to reinforce looking and attending to instructions, cooperation with the instructor's prompts and instructions, development of the child's imitative skills (if using sign language) or vocal imitation skills (if speaking), and attention to praise and changes in facial expression and tone of voice that precedes the delivery of the reinforcer. When teaching a skill involving the manipulation of blocks to match a model, the instructor can be developing the student's attention to the materials, independent completion of the task, coordination of fine motor movements, and looking for instructor feedback. Thus, it is possible for a well-trained instructor to teach the child how to listen, attend for longer periods of time, scan his environment, attend to more complex instructions and hopefully work for more naturally occurring social reinforcement in the process of trying to teach specific skills.

Although the skills are separated into different repertoire areas to ensure that the student can use the skills in a variety of situations, it is important to ensure that concepts are taught across all relevant repertoire areas (Lerman, Parten, Addison, Vorndran, Volkert, & Kodak, 2005; Wynn & Smith, 2003). For example, when teaching the concept of animals, it may be appropriate to include a variety of types of tasks to teach that concept. Specifically, the educational tasks may include sorting pictures of animals from non-animals (visual performance), receptively identifying animals, labeling pictures of various animals as "animal," requesting pictures of animals to complete a task, and learning to name a variety of animals when asked to "tell me some animals." The combination of learning activities can be varied across students, and must be designed based on the individual student's existing skills.

Teaching Academic Skills

As indicated above, many of the skills in the four Academic sections of *The ABLLS™-R Protocol* should generally not be of a higher priority than those in the Basic Learner Skills Section. This concern is especially critical for a child who does not have considerable skills in each of the basic learner areas. As with many traditional developmental norms (e.g., date first rolled over, walked), many parents and educators often use knowledge of body parts, colors, shapes, numbers and letters as indicators of a child's level of developmental progress. Unfortunately, these concepts are often more difficult to teach than many of the skills that the child may not have acquired (e.g., asking for reinforcing items and activities, receptively identifying and labeling common items he uses every day).

In some circumstances, a student may require several months of instruction before acquiring a difficult concept (e.g., the labels "blue" and "red"), when during that same period of time the child may have developed many easier skills that may have made it possible to teach the more difficult concept in a shorter amount of time. Another concern is when an emphasis is placed upon teaching academic skills that a young child will need in kindergarten (e.g., labeling numbers and letters) when the child is unable to receptively identify, request, label and talk about items that he uses on a daily basis (e.g., backpack, doors, windows, towels, soap, bowls). Without the development of many critical language skills, the academic skills may not be useful to the child, and will not help to ensure that the child will be able to learn new skills in a regular education classroom. Therefore, unless the child has made considerable progress in most of the areas of the Basic Learner Skills Section, or unless he already has easily learned some or has an interest in numbers, letters, etc., these types of skills should be deferred to a later time.

Teaching Self-Help Skills

Self-help skills are a part of everyday activities and are important skills to acquire. Therefore, the child's skills can be carefully shaped in the process of his participation in those activities. Many of the skills identified in the Basic Learner Skills section can be developed in conjunction with the teaching of the self-help skills. For example, the process of getting dressed can be a great opportunity to reinforce the child's cooperation, teach imitation (motor and vocal), teach him to request an item or activity, receptively identify and label items, and talk about those items. As such, a child should continue to develop self-help skills, but the overall focus of the skill development strategy should emphasize the development of language and other basic learner skills. It should be noted that the development of the child's cooperation during the teaching of basic language skills can make it easier to teach the child self-help skills as he participates in his daily routines.

Teaching Gross and Fine Motor Skills

As with self-help skills, there are many opportunities to incorporate the development of motor skills into many of the daily activities. The development of both fine and gross motor skills can also result in opportunities to reinforce the learner's cooperation, develop imitation, receptive language skills, following routines, etc. The development of these skills can also facilitate the development of social interaction skills (basic learner skills) by helping the child to learn to engage in motor activities that involve his peers. In situations where there are substantial motor deficits that interfere with the acquisition of other important skills, it is especially important to place an emphasis on the development of these skills. Motor skills can and should be incorporated into the instructional day in conjunction with, but not at the expense of, language and the other basic learner skills.

Strategies for Developing a Specific IEP

School-age children with severe language delays are most often provided educational services from the local school district. Although there may be a wide variation in services available from each school district, there is a federal requirement that each child with special needs have an Individualized Education Program (IEP).

The IEP is an important document in that it guides the focus of the educational activities and services provided for an individual child. In addition to specifying the type of educational environment in which services will be provided, it also contains specific learning objectives that are expected to be acquired over a period of time. Typically, the child's progress toward acquiring the skills specified in the IEP is reviewed each year. At the yearly review meeting, new objectives are selected for the coming year and services are arranged to facilitate the acquisition of the skills identified in the learning objectives. Therefore, it is extremely important that the focus of the child's educational program be clearly established in the learning objectives. An IEP is also an extremely valuable planning tool for children who are too young to qualify for public school services yet are in need of intervention.

Unfortunately, the objectives included in a child's IEP are often far from adequate to help ensure that the child will develop language and other critical learner skills. There are several sources of problems that occur in the development of the actual IEP. These problems typically involve the lack of an overall language-based curriculum to guide the selection of the objectives, a failure to adequately assess all of the basic learner skills, a failure to prioritize learning objectives, and a failure to write measurable objectives.

Considerable preparation is required in developing the learning objectives for a strategic teaching plan. The preparation should include a review of a child's skills in relationship to a curriculum that focuses on the development of language and other critical learner skills. Once the child's current skills are clearly delineated across all of the basic learner skill areas, it is then necessary to identify and prioritize the critical skills to be learned. Then, specific learning objectives must be written in a manner that all those involved with the child will be able to identify when the child has actually met an objective. As such, it is virtually impossible to develop an appropriate educational plan for a child with language delays without considerable preparation well in advance of the actual IEP meeting.

Overall Goal

The overall goal for the development of an IEP for a child with language delays is to develop a list of measurable objectives that adequately address the child's deficits in language and other basic learner skills (as per *The ABLLS™-R Protocol*). The plan should include both extending existing skills, but also ensuring that new skills are being developed. Additionally, if the child requires intensive educational services, the plan should ensure that skills are being developed that will eventually allow the child to learn in less-structured teaching situations, and from his everyday interactions.

Number of Objectives

It is important to consider the number of educational objectives–too many objectives can interfere with the quality of the necessary skills to be addressed, while too few objectives can often result in a failure to adequately address the needs of the learner. Too many or too few objectives are often indicative of a failure to realistically prioritize the necessary skills to be developed.

An effective IEP will most often contain 20–30 instructional objectives. Any one child is not likely to require objectives from all 25 skill areas of *The ABLLS™-R Protocol*. Typically, when one or two objectives are written for any of the 15 skill areas within the Basic Learner Skills Section, it is relatively easy to identify 20 appropriate instructional objectives. It is important to avoid an excessive number of objectives, as this will likely impact the training time available to ensure the development and acquisition of critical skills (in addition to the ability of the educational staff to effectively maintain and track each objective). Furthermore, it is important to allow time within the educational environment to accommodate opportunities for incidental teaching and to facilitate and promote generalization of the existing skills. The alternative to having an excessive amount of objectives is to add new learning tasks as the existing objectives are met.

Content of the IEP

The selection of educational objectives for an individual child must be based upon the unique needs of the child. As such, it is impossible to specify exact criteria for the selection of objectives for children. However, it is possible to provide some general guidelines to help with the selection process. It is also possible to obtain additional suggestions for a particular child by reviewing the recommendations for teaching language in the book, *Teaching Language to Children With Autism or Other Developmental Disabilities* (Sundberg & Partington, 1998). A review of some general guidelines will be presented in a manner that corresponds with the four major sections of *The ABLLS™-R Protocol*: Basic Learner Skills, Academic Skills, Self-Help Skills, and Motor Skills.

Basic Learner Skills

The overall goal of the educational program for the child with language delays should be that he learns language and other basic learner skills that will allow him to be able to learn from his everyday activities. In general, the amount of time spent on educational activities should be allocated in correspondence with the importance of the skills to be acquired (Payne, Radicchi, Rosellini, Deutchman, & Darch, 1983). Because the Basic Learner Skills section of *The ABLLS™-R* provides a basis for a curriculum that emphasizes language and other skills to be an effective learner, the majority of instructional objectives should be derived from this section.

It is generally recommended that at least one half to two thirds of the objectives are selected from the Basic Learner Skills Section. Depending upon the child's skills in each of the areas of this section, the development of some of the 15 skill areas may require several objectives, while other skill areas may not require any objectives at the present time. A review of some guidelines for each of the skill areas of the Basic Learner Skills section is provided below.

A. Cooperation and Reinforcer Effectiveness

It is very important to develop the child's cooperation and to gradually thin the schedule of reinforcement for participation in learning tasks. However, it is often not necessary to include a specific objective for the thinning of the reinforcement schedule because the cooperation of the student and his ability to work for less direct reinforcement is often a direct byproduct of good teaching practices. However, if the child has difficulty responding to instructor-controlled reinforcers, to intermittent reinforcement schedules, to social reinforcers, or to a variety of instructors, it may be beneficial to include an objective from this area.

It is also important to ensure that the child is able to participate in tasks presented at tables. Therefore, if the child does not sit appropriately, wait without handling the educational materials, watch and listen for instructions, then scan the materials and complete the specified task in a timely manner, it would be appropriate to include objectives to help ensure the acquisition of those skills.

B. Visual Performance

It is often beneficial to include one to three objectives from the visual performance area. Many children with language delays show considerable strength in attending to and manipulating nonverbal stimuli. As such, objectives can be selected to build on a child's existing strengths so he can easily obtain reinforcement for participation in learning activities while developing his ability to attend to increasing complex arrays of stimuli.

The development of visual performance skills often results in the development of other critical skills. For example when a child learns to complete a puzzle, he may become more cooperative with responding to the instructor's physical prompts and verbal instructions, may learn to work until the task is completed (without prompts to continue), and may develop better fine motor skills.

C. Receptive Language

It is usually critical to include at least one or more objectives from this skill area. Receptive language is almost always in need of development even for children who have strengths in this area compared to other language areas.

If the child does not follow simple directions, or is unable to select a named item from a simple display of items, it would be important to include an objective to develop each of those skills. For example, it may be appropriate to include an objective to follow simple instructions in the context of daily activities, and another to be able to discriminate five to ten items presented in an array of two items. For the child who can follow a few instructions and can receptively identify five to ten items, it may be appropriate to include objectives to follow more complex directions, to receptively identify a greater number of items (perhaps 30 to 50 total items), or to receptively identify actions.

When setting the criterion for objectives it is beneficial to specify the total number of known items, rather than specifying that the child will "learn 30 new items." It is usually easier to specify the total number of items a child can identify than it is to determine how many of those items have been learned since the previous IEP meeting.

For the child who can discriminate over 50 to 100 items, it may be appropriate to include objectives to learn complex receptive discrimination with verbs, adjective-noun combinations, prepositions, noun-verb combinations, etc. It may also be beneficial to include an objective for the child to be able to receptively identify items when told something about the item (i.e., receptive by function, feature or class), or to follow instructions that require him to follow more complex instructions across time and space (e.g., go get the cup from the kitchen table).

D. Motor Imitation

In general, an imitation objective should be included for any child who does not have well-developed and generalized imitative repertoire. It is critical that the child be able to match a wide variety of actions including those that are held in a static (constant) position (e.g., palms held together, and those that are kinetic (involve motion) responses (e.g., clapping hands). It is also important that the child be able to match the speed and intensity of actions and to be able to switch actions when others switch to a new action. The development of motor imitation skills can help develop the student's ability to attend to an instruction for a longer period of time and to attend to the dynamic characteristics of the required responses. The development of the ability to pay close attention to the details of **how** a response is made can help facilitate the development of the imitation of vocalizations (Ross & Greer 2003). If the student only needs to learn to imitate peers or to engage in spontaneous imitation, these skills can be addressed in an objective listed under the social skills or play skills area.

E. Vocal Imitation (Echoics)

An objective to improve vocal imitation is usually appropriate to consider for a child does not have clear speech. For the child who can not echo words, it may be beneficial to target simple vocalizations (maybe only 2 sounds) and target head and mouth imitation (if those skills are also weak). For the child can echo sounds, it is often beneficial to target simple combinations of sounds, simple words and/or phrases. For the child who can repeat phrases, it may be appropriate to include objectives that focus on improving articulation or the variation in volume, tone, or the speed of the child's speech (i.e., prosody).

F. Requests (Mands)

Most children with language delays need to improve their ability to request reinforcers and information. For a child who does not specifically request items or activities, it is important to include at least one objective for the child to be able to ask for several items and/or activities, and another objective to spontaneously request those items and activities. For the child who can spontaneously ask for a variety of items and activities, it would be appropriate to include objectives for the child to ask for missing items (e.g., a crayon to draw on paper), for information (e.g., "who," "what," and "where" questions), and for items from peers (vs. adults). It should be noted that this latter objective could also be included under the social skills section of the IEP. Finally, it is important to remember that a child should look at others when requesting items and activities.

G. Labeling (Tacts)

As with receptive language, it is almost always critical to include at least one or more objectives on labeling. Labeling skills are always in need of development even for children who have strengths in this area compared to other language areas. If the child cannot label any items, but does have the ability to repeat words or to imitate American Sign Language signs (ASL), it would be important to include an objective to develop these skills. For example, it may be appropriate to include an objective to label at least five items (e.g., reinforcers or common items).

For the child who can label five to ten items, it may be appropriate to include objectives to label a greater number of items (perhaps 30 to 50 total items). A child who can label 50 to 100 items may benefit from the inclusion of objectives to learn more complex labeling skills including verbs, noun-verb combinations, adjective-noun combinations, prepositions, pronouns, etc.

H. Intraverbals

Objectives to teach intraverbal skills are usually appropriate for a vocal child who can request at least a few items or activities, and has some labeling and receptive language skills. For a child with these skills, it may be appropriate to include an objective to fill in words from songs or to fill in words to complete simple phrases. For a nonvocal child who is learning to request at least a few items using American Sign Language (ASL), it may be appropriate to include a single objective to make a specific sign upon request (i.e., ASL translation).

A child who can receptively identify and label over 100 items and actions should have several objectives to address the development of his intraverbal skills. These objectives should probably include skills such as describing sequences of actions to complete activities; the functions, features, and classification of items; and answering a variety of "wh" questions.

I. Spontaneous Vocalizations

It is very important to develop the child's spontaneous vocalizations. However, it is often not necessary to include a specific objective for this area because spontaneous language often increases as a direct result of the naturally-occurring reinforcement of using language. However, if the child has acquired numerous language skills but does not spontaneously use those skills, it may be beneficial to include an objective from this area, and to review the motivational factors related to the use of the student's skills. It is important to remember that many language skills are maintained by social reinforcement, especially language that does not involve requesting items, actions, or information. As such, it is important to ensure that the student's spontaneous language (not including requests) actually results in reinforcement.

J. Syntax and Grammar

When a child has developed requesting, labeling, and intraverbal skills and is starting to combine words (or ASL) into phrases, it may be appropriate to include an objective or two for this area. Many syntax and grammar skills are developed in the process of learning more advanced requesting, labeling, and intraverbal skills as models of appropriate word order are continuously provided as people interact with the child (Palmer, 1996; Palmer 1998). However, it is important to not over-emphasize the development of these formal aspects of language until each of the functional language skills is well established.

K. Play/Leisure Skills

It is usually appropriate to include at least one objective to increase a child's play or leisure skills. For the child who does not play with toys or engage in appropriate leisure activities, it is usually desirable to have an objective to increase the variety of play activities, and perhaps a second objective to increase the amount of time spent in play or leisure activities. For a child who does have some appropriate play and leisure skills, it is often appropriate to include an objective to engage in play and leisure skills that include interactions with peers.

L. Social Interaction Skills

Social interaction skills are always in need of development for children, regardless of their language skills. If the child has very weak language skills, then returning greetings, turn-taking, approaching others for interactions, and giving up reinforcers are important social skills to target. If the child has a variety of language skills, then he can learn to request items or information from peers, make offers to share, initiate greetings, converse with others, and learn to talk about topics of interest to others.

It is also critical that a child learn to attend to the actions and interests of others. There is a considerable amount of subtle changes in our behavior that can provide feedback to a child regarding the appropriateness of his behavior, as well as the potential for desired and undesired consequences. In order to be successful in interacting with others, it is important to teach the child to attend to these subtle changes in the spoken words, the manner in which the words are spoken, the facial expressions, and the actions of others.

The motivational variables associated with a child's interest in interacting with others must also be considered. The child may have the language skills to interact with others. However, if the child's interaction with others does not result in reinforcement, the child may gain access to other reinforcers that do not require social interaction.

M. Group Instruction

It is usually appropriate to include at least one objective to develop a child's group participation skills. An exception to this recommendation would occur when a child does not respond to instructions or educational activities unless instructions are presented directly to him. Another exception would be a child who exhibits a high rate of aggressive behavior when near peers.

For a child with minimal language and group participation skills, instructional objectives may only target the use of known skills in small groups (e.g., imitation, or simple receptive and labeling tasks).

For a child with more advanced language and group participation skills, group instruction objectives should target acquiring new language skills (e.g., tact and/or intraverbal) in groups, and participation in groups of a larger size. When writing objectives to teach group skills, it is important to specify the ratio of teacher to students required to meet the objective, and to specify the types of responses to be required from the child.

N. Classroom Routines

It is frequently appropriate to include an objective to address the development of following classroom routines. These objectives often play a crucial role in the development of basic receptive skills, and may be important for a child who engages in disruptive behavior during transitions between activities. Objectives in this area are particularly important to help prepare a student for transition into another classroom that has established routines and expectations for all students.

P. Generalized Responding

Because the generalization of skills is typically a standard part of the development of specific skills, it is not always necessary to include an objective to address generalization. However, if a child has difficulty in generalizing his skills (i.e., he only learns each response in extremely controlled situations), it may be appropriate to include an objective to ensure generalization is part of the plan.

Q-T. Academic Skills

As mentioned previously, educational objectives for academic skills are often not as critical as the objectives derived to address the skills included in the Basic Learner Skills section of *The ABLLS™-R*. However, for the child who has developed skills in most of the Basic Learner Skills Section, it is appropriate to consider an objective or two from each of the academic areas. For a child who has not developed many of the basic learner skills but who demonstrates a high interest in numbers, letters, or words, it may be appropriate to identify one or two objectives that correspond to the child's interest.

U-X. Self-Help Skills

For a child who has difficulty with self-help skills or other activities of daily living, it is often appropriate to select one or more objectives to teach the necessary dressing, eating, grooming or toileting skills. However, rather than devoting a large amount of the instructional day to teaching these skills, it is often more appropriate to teach these skills in the context of the normal, daily activities. The development of these skills also provides a great context for teaching and generalizing the basic learner skills.

Motor Skills

Y. Gross Motor

If a child has any gross motor skills deficits, it is usually desirable to include an objective or two that focuses on the development of those skills (significant delays in motor skills should be reviewed by an appropriate professional, i.e., neurologist, occupational therapist, etc.). For a child with minimal language skills and minimal receptive instruction-following skills, or students with weak coordination or muscle control, it is often desirable to have several specific objectives to address each skill to be taught. For a child who has more advanced language and motor skills, it is often possible to combine several related skills into a single objective (e.g., the child will be able to roll, throw, and kick a ball at a target).

The development of motor skills is very important for helping the child be a successful participant in social interactions and mainstreaming opportunities (e.g., playing games on a playground). As such, it may be desirable to include a gross motor skill that involves peers in this section or under the social interaction section of the IEP.

Z. Fine Motor

It may be appropriate to include objectives to increase a child's fine motor skills; however, many fine motor skills are often addressed under other sections of the IEP. For example, for a child with only minimal language skills, some fine motor skills will be developed while the child works on the objectives in the visual performance section of the IEP (e.g., putting blocks onto block design cards). If that same child already has some gross motor imitation skills, or will allow physical prompting, it may be desirable to pick a few simple tasks to be acquired. A child with more advanced basic learner skills may have fine motor skills developed in the process of learning skills included under the academics section (e.g., a tracing or writing letters objective).

Behavioral Issues

Although *The ABLLS™-R* does not specifically address disruptive behaviors, it is important to include objectives to address these concerns. Including objectives to address behavioral concerns will help ensure that appropriate interventions are developed to reduce undesired behaviors by teaching appropriate or incompatible behaviors. In many situations, it is important to gain the involvement of a behavior specialist, and that can only be arranged if there is a specific need identified in the IEP objectives. There are many factors that influence the occurrence of disruptive behavior including the difficulty of the task, the number of responses required to gain access to a reinforcer, and the availability of other reinforcers for alternative behaviors. As such, when a child exhibits disruptive behavior, it is important to seek a well-trained behavioral consultant to help identify the function of the behavior of concern and to recommend appropriate intervention strategies (input from behavioral consultants who are certified through the Behavior Analyst Certification Board (www.bacb.com) will provide assurance that the consultants have had formal training and supervision in behavior analysis). Even when the behavior of concern has improved, it is often helpful to include a behavioral maintenance objective to remind those who are working with the child of the need to attend to the effective strategies that were implemented to change the undesired behavior.

Input From Others

When developing an IEP, it is important to consider input from a variety of individuals who are familiar with the child's existing skills. Although *The ABLLS™-R Protocol* provides a considerable amount of information regarding the child's skills, it is very important to ensure the appropriateness of the objectives selected for the child. It is beneficial to discuss the proposed objectives with, and get input from, all individuals associated with the child (e.g., parents, educators, speech and language pathologists, occupational therapists, behavior analysts, psychologists, or developmental pediatricians) prior to holding the IEP meeting. A review by several knowledgeable individuals will help to ensure that the proposed learning plan is reasonable and includes all skills that should be addressed in the plan. The review by a well-trained team of parents and professionals can help ensure that reasonable expectations are being made regarding the likely outcomes for the child's development as he progresses through his long-term educational plan.

Criteria

Once the objectives have been selected to ensure that critical skills have been identified in the child's plan, it is then necessary to ensure that there is agreement as to how the student will demonstrate the skill that was acquired. Although there are differing methods for measuring acquisition (e.g., 8 out of 10 trials, 80% accuracy), the important consideration is that all individuals reach agreement as to the level of performance expected for each skill. In the situation where the classroom staff are already using adequate data collection procedures, it is often sufficient to utilize existing standards for the collection of acquisition data. However, if the staff are not accustomed to collecting data, or their methods of data collection are inadequate for the identified skills, it is often necessary to clearly delineate the conditions under which the skill is expected to be demonstrated and the exact method for measuring the level of performance.

Rather than specify and collect data on every aspect of a particular skill, it is often possible to minimize the negative impact of collecting "too much data" on staff by including teacher observation criteria for objectives such as self-help, classroom routines, and motor skills. "Teacher observation" is often adequate in situations where the members of the child's IEP team clearly understand the level of performance that is expected (e.g., the child will be able to independently wash and dry his hands). However, how the skill will be developed should be discussed to ensure that there is agreement as to what is meant by the objective (e.g., wash hands with soap, without another child or adult standing next to the child, dry hands with paper towels from a dispenser).

When competent specialists are contracted to provide certain educational services, it is often helpful to allow that person to recommend the criterion of performance desired for the skills that they are to develop. For example, many professionals such as speech and language pathologists, adaptive physical education specialists, and occupational therapists, have well-established methods of documenting the progress of certain skills. Whenever their methods of measuring progress are sufficient for the other members of the IEP team to determine whether progress is occurring, it is unnecessary to require them to alter their routines. It is important to remember that the emphasis should be on the development of the child's skills, rather than on the level of specificity included in a written document.

Review of ABLLS™-R Profiles

In order to apply the general guidelines for developing educational priorities for a particular child, descriptions of the skills of two fictitious children will be presented and analyzed (any resemblance to a specific child is merely coincidental). These same profiles will also be used to demonstrate how to develop a specific IEP using the information obtained from *The ABLLS™-R* (it is not recommended that these examples be used for an actual child's IEP without completely reviewing an individual child's needs).

The first profile will be of an "Early Learner" who lacks language skills and most of the other basic learner skills. The second profile will be of a more "Advanced Learner" who has acquired some, but not all, of the basic learner skills. A completed skills tracking grid and a set of recommended IEP objectives for each of the learner profiles can be found in Appendices 2 and 3, respectively.

Review of an "Early Learner" ABLLS™-R Profile

General Description

Sarah is 3 years, 3 months of age. Her parents have been concerned about her failure to speak since she was about 30 months of age, and they have taken her to several specialists to determine the nature of her language delay. Her parents describe Sarah as a happy little girl who entertains herself, and who does not appear to care about the activities of others. She was given a diagnosis of autistic disorder just prior to her third birthday. She has recently been enrolled in a school that specializes in providing early intervention services to young children with autism. The program is an intensive, behaviorally-based, language program. A blend of discrete trial and natural environment training is provided to her. Sarah's parents are active participants in her education. Since she started the program, she has begun to acquire a variety of skills.

Early Learner Assessment Sections A-D

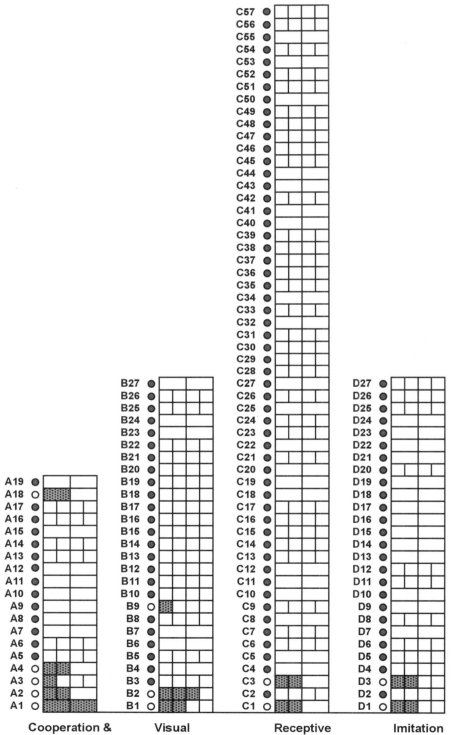

**Cooperation &
Reinforcer
Effectiveness**

**Visual
Performance**

**Receptive
Language**

Imitation

Assessment of Skills

   The ABLLS™-R was used to determine Sarah's skills in each of the 25 areas of the assessment. A description of her skills will be presented (see page 42 for the results of her performance presented on the skills tracking grids for each of the skill areas), followed by an analysis of those skills to determine the priorities for her educational program. Additionally, a review of the rationale for the selection of recommended specific learning objectives for Sarah will be provided.

Basic Learner Skills Section

A. Cooperation and Reinforcer Effectiveness

   Sarah will usually take a preferred item and will sometimes accept a common item when it is handed to her (A1=2, A2-4=1). She will occasionally look to see if someone has noticed something that she has done (A18=1).

B. Visual Performance

   Sarah is unable to match identical objects, nor identical pictures (B3-7=0). She has recently learned to match two colored blocks to a pattern on a design card (B9=1), and to complete several single-piece inset puzzles (B1=2) and place a few blocks into a form box when the pieces are individually handed to her (B2=3).

C. Receptive Language

   Sarah will sometimes look at a person when her name is called (C1=1) and will occasionally follow an instruction to look at objects that are held in front of her (C3=1). She does not follow simple directions without prompts (C2 & 4-7=0) and is unable to receptively identify objects (C11-14=0).

D. Imitation

   Sarah does not attend to nor spontaneously imitate the actions of others (D26=0). She has recently learned to imitate 8 motor actions (D3=2) and 8 actions (D1=2) using objects (e.g., pounding a drum).   She is unable to imitate any actions involving her head, mouth, or tongue (D9&10=0).

Early Learner Assessment Sections E-K

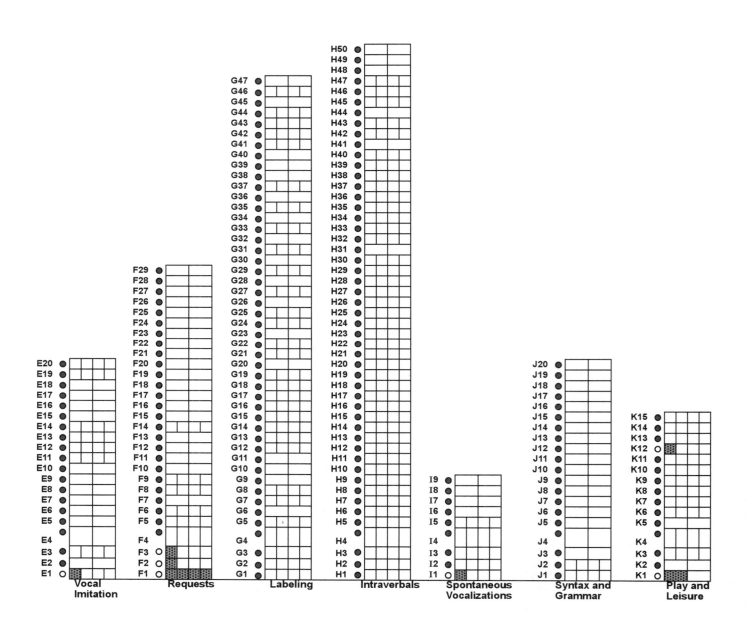

E. Vocal Imitation

Sarah has just started imitating two sounds "mmm" and "aaa." She cannot imitate any other sounds or words (E1=1).

F. Requests

Sarah indicates that she wants a particular item or activity by standing next to the item she wants (F1=2). She has recently learned to use American Sign Language (ASL) to ask for candy and books (she likes to look at the pictures). She will only use her newly-acquired requesting skills when the items are present and she is asked, "What do you want?" (F2&3=1, F4=0).

G. Labeling

Sarah does not know the names of any items (All G=0).

H. Intraverbals

Sarah is unable to talk and does not have enough skills with ASL to be able to engage in conversational activities, and she cannot she fill in the words of simple songs, phrases, or word associations (all H=0).

I. Spontaneous Vocalizations

Sarah is a very quiet girl and rarely babbles or makes any speech sounds (I1=1).

J. Syntax and Grammar

With the exception of using single ASL signs to ask for two items, Sarah does not communicate (All J=0).

K. Play/Leisure Skills

Sarah does explore some toys for a few minutes at a time (K1=2) and can throw a ball (K12=1), but she does not use the toys as they were designed, unless she receives multiple physical prompts from an adult (K5=0).

Early Learner Assessment Sections L-S

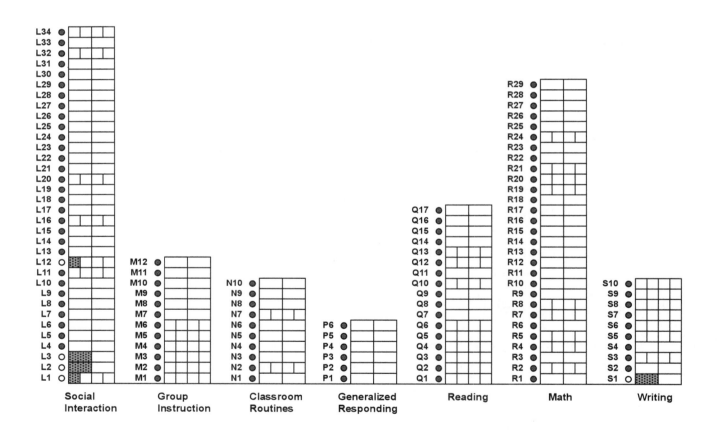

L. Social Interaction Skills

Sarah does not initiate social interactions with peers (L4-6=0), but occasionally she will allow other children to guide her to an activity (L1, 3, & 12=1), and she will occasionally take items that are offered to her (L2=1).

M. Group Instruction

Sarah does not attend well to instructions that are presented directly to her and wanders away from all attempts to engage her in a group activity (all M=0).

N. Classroom Routines

Sarah does not follow any classroom routines such as putting away her materials, or hanging-up her backpack upon arrival at school (all N=0).

P. Generalized Responding

The few skills that Sarah has acquired only occur in the exact situation in which the skill was initially taught (all P=0).

Academic Skills

Q. Reading

Sarah cannot identify any words or letters (all Q=0).

R. Math

Sarah cannot count or recognize any numbers (all R=0).

S. Writing

Sarah is able to mark on paper when a crayon and paper are given to her (S1=1), but she is unable to color between lines (S2=0), or to trace or copy any specific markings or write any letters (S3-8=0).

T. Spelling

Sarah is unable to spell (all T=0).

Early Learner Assessment Sections T-Z

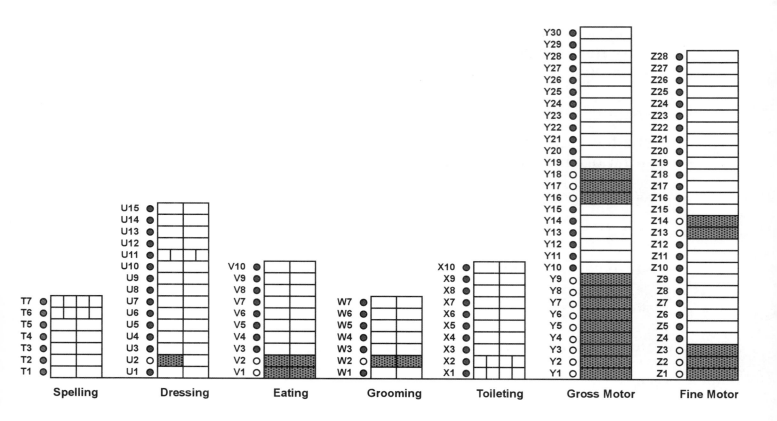

Self-Help Skills

U. Dressing Skills

Sarah can remove her shoes (U2=1), but otherwise does not help with any dressing activities (U1&3-15=0).

V. Eating Skills

Sarah can put food items in her mouth by using her fingers (V1=2) and drinks liquids from a straw (V2=2). She cannot use utensils or drink from a cup without spilling (V3&4=0).

W. Grooming

Sarah is unable to wash her hands (W1=0), but she will independently take a paper towel and wipe her hands after her hands have been washed for her (W2=2).

X. Toileting

Sarah wears diapers and has never eliminated in a toilet (all X=0).

Motor Skills

Y. Gross Motor Skills

Sarah can walk forwards and backwards, kneel, run smoothly, jump forward and down from objects (Y1-7=1). She can also hop (Y8=1), throw a ball (Y9=1), and ride a tricycle (Y16=1).

Z. Fine Motor Skills

Sarah can do a variety of fine motor activities such as place objects in a form box (Z2), simple single-piece inset puzzles (Z3=1), stack blocks (Z13=1), string beads (Z14=1), and mark on paper with a crayon (Z1=1).

Educational Priorities for Sarah

In developing an educational program for Sarah, the emphasis should be on developing her willingness and ability to engage in a variety of instructor-controlled activities, and in her ability to use language skills. She will need to learn to attend to a variety of visual stimuli and instructions presented to her by her instructors. Her cooperation in the learning process is crucial. Therefore, in order to increase the amount of time she participates in instructor-controlled activities, it is essential to create and/or capture her motivation.

One of the most effective methods of establishing her participation in the activities is to teach her to request (i.e., mand) highly reinforcing items or activities. By teaching a child to request reinforcers, in addition to learning to ask for specific items and activities, reinforcement is also provided for attending to items being held by others, approaching people for social interaction, attending to the actions of others, imitation of actions, and following instructions. Procedures for establishing the cooperation by teaching requesting (i.e., manding) skills are delineated in the book, *Teaching Language to Children with Autism or Other Developmental Disabilities* (Sundberg & Partington, 1998).

An IEP has been developed for Sarah based on the review of her skills provided by *The ABLLS™-R* (See Appendix 2). Specific learning objectives were identified for Sarah (see page 51). Objectives were included in several of the skill areas in *The ABLLS™-R*, primarily from the Basic Learner Skills section of the assessment.

There were no specific objectives included regarding increasing cooperation because her cooperation will be directly shaped in the development of other skills (e.g., requesting skills). Objectives from the visual performance section included further development of her ability to place blocks on block design cards (Objective 1), completion of simple puzzles (Objective 2), and teaching the new skill of matching identical items and identical pictures to a display that includes the matching item or picture (Objectives 3 & 4). A few objectives were included from the receptive language section including the ability to follow instructions to do a specified motor task (e.g., "arms up") (Objective 5) and to receptively select a named item from a display of reinforcing or common items (e.g., "Give me cup") (Objective 6). Several objectives were

"Early Learner" Objectives

1. Sarah will be able to match blocks to a design card for up to 5 blocks with no extra blocks.

2. Sarah will be able to complete at least 5 interlocking puzzles in a frame with 5 pieces or more.

3. When presented with an array of three or more objects and given an object that matches one of those in the display, Sarah will match the object to the appropriate object.

4. When presented with an array of three or more pictures and given an object that is in one of the pictures, Sarah will match the object to the appropriate picture for any picture/object combination.

5. Sarah will follow instructions to do at least 6 simple motor tasks (e.g., clap, turn around, arms up).

6. Sarah will be able to receptively identify at least 10 items.

7. Sarah will be able to imitate 15 actions with objects when they are modeled and when instructed to "Do this."

8. Sarah will be able to imitate at least 20 gross motor actions (e.g., clap hands, touch tummy, etc.) when they are modeled and when instructed to "Do this."

9. Sarah will be able to imitate at least 5 head, mouth, and/or tongue movements when they are modeled and when instructed to "Do this."

10. Sarah will imitate at least 5 different sounds upon request.

(Continued on page 53)

recommended for the further development of her motoric (Objectives 7- 9) and vocal imitative skills (Objective 10). It is important to develop imitation skills that require her to attend to matching both visual and auditory patterns of responding. Vocal speech should be the primary goal of her language training program. However, because she is not readily imitating vocal speech, the development of her ability to imitate motor actions will facilitate her ability to communicate using ASL (i.e., requesting, labeling, intraverbal), while she also learns the more difficult skill of learning to vocally imitate sounds and words.

As mentioned previously, one of the major elements of her program must include teaching her to request reinforcing items and activities. She must learn to ask for a variety of reinforcers (Objective 11) and must receive reinforcement for spontaneously requesting those reinforcers (Objective 12).

After she is able to specifically request a variety of items, it will also be important for her to learn to be able to label (i.e., tact) those items. Therefore, an objective was included to ensure that she learns to label items either using vocal speech or ASL (Objective 13).

Because she does not engage in many spontaneous vocalizations, it is important to directly reinforce her vocalizations, especially speech types of sounds. Thus, an objective has been included to ensure that those who interact with Sarah will watch for opportunities to prompt and reinforce her vocalizations, including those that are non-imitative (Objective 14).

Objectives were established to increase her play skills and her interactions with peers. Directly teaching her ways in which to use toys in a manner that is similar to typically-developing peers will allow greater opportunities to interact with her peers (Objective 15). Additionally teaching her to roll a ball to a peer will extend her motor skills (i.e., she can already throw and catch a ball), will directly shape her attending to the actions of her peers, and will reinforce her for following socially-oriented routines (Objective 16).

The last specific learning objective from the Basic Learner Skills section involves following classroom routines. It is important

"Early Learner" Objectives (continued)

11. Sarah will be able to request at least 10 different items through the use of sign language or vocalizations.

12. Sarah will request desired items by sign language or vocalizations at least 10 times per day.

13. Sarah will be able to label at least 10 items using sign language or vocalizations. This objective is to be started once Sarah can request and receptively identify at least 10 objects.

14. Sarah will increase her spontaneous vocalizations that include speech sounds by 50% over baseline levels.

15. Sarah will be able to play with at least 5 different toys as designed for at least 2 minutes with no more than 2 physical prompts.

16. Sarah will roll a ball to another peer or adult for at least 3 exchanges.

17. Sarah will complete her morning routine (e.g., hang up her coat, put lunch box in cubbie, put away backpack), with no more than 2 verbal prompts.

18. Sarah will be able to pull down her pants without assistance (to help with the toileting process).

19. Sarah will be able to wash her hands without assistance.

20. Sarah will be able to trace straight lines.

for Sarah to observe and imitate consistent daily classroom activities. Therefore, an objective is included to teach her to engage in typical classroom activities without requiring prompts from instructors (e.g., hang up her coat upon arrival, put her lunch in the appropriate location, and then go to a designated area) (Objective 17).

There are four areas of the Basic Learner Skills section that were not appropriate for specific objectives at this time. Because she does not speak and does not know many ASL signs for items, there were no objectives for intraverbal skills (e.g., conversation) or for syntax and grammar skills. Additionally, because she does not attend except when instructions are presented directly to her, there are currently no objectives recommended to increase her group participation skills. These skills will be initially established by increasing her skills in following classroom routines and through the social interaction objectives. The generalized responding section is the final skill area that does not have a specific learning objective. The reason for not including a specific objective at this time is that the learner will be generalizing some of her skills both through the specific instruction to teach the other objectives (e.g., she will be learning a generalized imitative repertoire), and because she will be generalizing her skills by using them in a variety of locations at home and school, and using them with a variety of individuals (i.e., various instructors and her parents).

Although self-help skills should not be the major focus of her educational program, development of these skills during the normal course of her daily activities would be appropriate. Many basic learner skills (e.g., attending to visual stimuli, following routines, following simple directions) would be strengthened while learning to do certain skills that must occur on a daily basis. Therefore, specific objectives were included to teach her to pull down her pants when taken to the toilet (Objective 18), and to wash her hands (especially since she can already dry her hands) (Objective 19).

Because of Sarah's needs to develop the basic learner skills, attempting to develop reading, math, and spelling skills would be inappropriate. However, because she can mark on a paper when given a crayon, it would be reasonable to teach her to visually attend to lines and patterns on a paper by learning to trace simple straight lines (Objective 20). This activity would also result in improvements in her fine motor skills.

Review of an "Advanced Learner" ABLLS™-R Profile

General Description

Jason is 5 years, 2 months of age. He was enrolled in an early intervention program for children with developmental delays when he was 28 months of age and was given a diagnosis of autistic disorder when he was three and a half years old. Jason was enrolled in a special education class for children with developmental disabilities for one year. During that time, he received consultation from a speech and language pathologist. One year ago, he was enrolled in an educational program that specializes in providing services to young children with autism. The school is an intensive, behaviorally-based, language program that uses a blend of discrete-trial and natural environment training. Since he started in his new classroom, Jason has begun to acquire a variety of skills.

Assessment of Skills

The ABLLS™-R was used to determine Jason's skills in the 25 skill areas in the assessment. A description of his skills in each of the areas will be presented (see page 56 for the results of his performance presented on the skills tracking grids for each of the skill areas), followed by an analysis of those skills to determine the priorities for his educational program. Additionally, a review of the rationale for the selection of recommended specific learning objectives for the learner is provided.

Basic Learner Skills Section

A. Cooperation and Reinforcer Effectiveness

Jason is fairly easy to motivate in teaching situations (A1-6=maximum scores). He will work equally well for a variety of instructors (A7=2) and will work well with materials at a table (A8, &9-11=2, A10=1). Although he does not look at the instructors' faces after responding to an instruction (A15 & 18=0) and the completion of tasks does not serve as a reinforcer for his activities (A19=0), he will readily work for a variety of edible and activity reinforcers. His responding in teaching

Advanced Learner Assessment Sections A-C

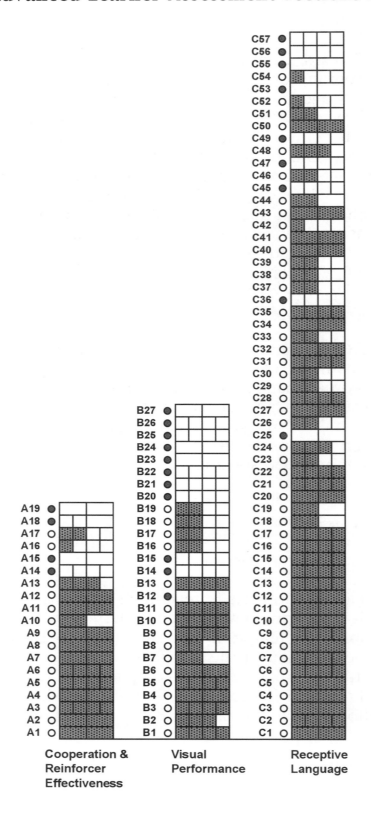

**Cooperation &
Reinforcer
Effectiveness**

**Visual
Performance**

**Receptive
Language**

activities can usually be maintained by providing praise for each correct response and when followed by a back-up reinforcer after approximately every three or four responses (A13=3 & A16=1). He does have difficulty in teaching situations when the delivery of a reinforcer is delayed for more than about 20 seconds (A17=2). This inability to wait for a reinforcer presents problems in that he will engage in disruptive behavior during teaching sessions, especially in small group instruction where the rate of reinforcement is often decreased due to the teacher's need to work with the other students in the group.

B. Visual Performance

Jason can match both identical objects and pictures (B3&5=4, B4&6=2). He has recently learned to match up to six colored blocks to a pattern on a design card (B9=4) and match a sequence pattern using those same blocks (B13=4). He is unable to make a visual pattern when the sample pattern is presented in a picture (B12=0), and he cannot extend the sequence beyond that of the original model (B22=0). Jason can complete single-piece inset puzzles (B1=4) and complete several eight-piece puzzles that have a frame into which the pieces are placed (B10&11=4). Jason is unable to complete puzzles that do not have a frame (B14&15=0).

C. Receptive Language

Jason has quite extensive receptive language skills. He is able to follow many simple directions (C1-15= maximum scores), and is able to receptively identify over 150 common objects and pictures (C16&17=4). He can also receptively identify over 20 actions, either by demonstrating the action (C34=2), or by selecting pictures representing the action (C35=4). Jason is able to take items to a specified location or person (C28=4), but is unable to independently get requested items from a specified person or location (C29=2). He is only able to receptively select a few items when told the item's function, one of its features, or the class to which the item belongs (C37-39=2). Jason can receptively identify examples of three prepositions (C51=2) and two pronouns (C52=1). He can receptively identify seven colors and five non-color adjectives (C24=3).

Advanced Learner Assessment Sections D-H

D. Imitation

Jason can imitate most simple gross and fine motor actions (D1-8=maximum scores, D9&10=1) but has difficulty imitating a sequence of actions (D20=1). He also has difficulty matching the speed of the modeled actions (D16&17=1).

E. Vocal Imitation

Jason can fairly accurately imitate most words and phrases of up to four words (E1-12=maximum scores, E13=3). He will spontaneously imitate phrases he hears (E20=3), but often his vocal imitations do not match the speed (e.g., fast vs. slow), volume or pitch of the model (E15-17=0).

F. Requests

Jason can and does request a variety of desired items and activities throughout the day including items that are not currently within sight (F1-7=maximum scores). However, he does not request items necessary to complete a task (F9=1) and does not ask for information other than occasionally asking for the name of an item (F19=2, F20&21=0, F24-28=0). Jason can ask for paper when he wants to draw a picture.

G. Labeling

Jason can label over 150 items and over 10 actions (G1-5=4, G6=2, G7&8=3). He is unable to label items using adjectives other than the color of the item (G13=2). When given a display of several items and told one of the item's functions or features, he is able to correctly label only two or three items (G15&16=2). He is unable to label an item from a display when told the class to which the item belongs (G17=0).

H. Intraverbals

Although he can name over 150 items and can label some actions, Jason engages in almost no conversation about items that are not present. He will fill in a few words from one or two songs (H1=1), and knows the sounds of four animals (i.e., a dog

Advanced Learner Assessment Sections I-M

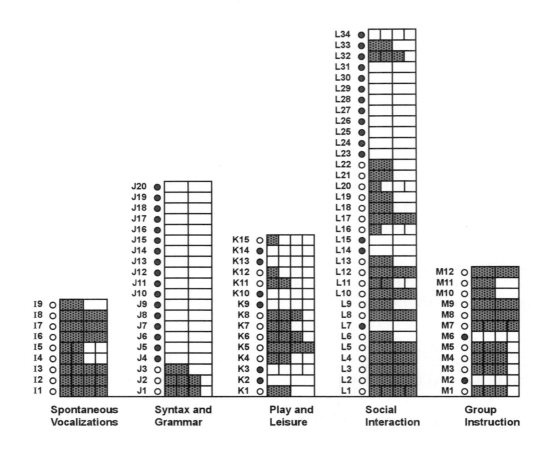

Spontaneous Vocalizations   **Syntax and Grammar**   **Play and Leisure**   **Social Interaction**   **Group Instruction**

says _____) (H4=2). He can give his first name and age when asked (H5=2), and can fill in the function of approximately five items (e.g., you use scissors to _____) (H8&9=2). Jason cannot identify the categories of items (H14&18=0) or discuss the features of items (H16&17=0).

I. Spontaneous vocalizations

Jason uses his language skills consistently throughout the day (I1-3=4). He will spontaneously ask for items and activities (I7=2), label items (I8=2), and adds some relevant statements during ongoing conversations (I9=1), typically about an item that is within his sight.

J. Syntax and Grammar

Although his sentences are short, Jason typically combines his words in a correct sequence. He will usually combine an article and either a verb or an adjective with a noun (J2=3, J3=1). His statements do not indicate past or future tense (J6,9&13=0), and he does not use plurals (J5=0).

K. Play/Leisure Skills

Jason plays with a variety of toys as they were designed (K5&7=2), and makes frequent comments about his play activities (K6=3). He will share his toys with children when they ask to use his play items (K8=3).

L. Social Interaction Skills

Jason initiates social interactions with both peers and adults (L5=2) and will also will respond to social interactions initiated by others (L8&12=2). He will consistently return greetings from both adults and peers (L10=2) but he often requires prompts to initiate greetings to his peers (L21=1). Jason seeks to interact with others but will usually not make multiple attempts to get a peer to interact with him (L6=2, L20=1).

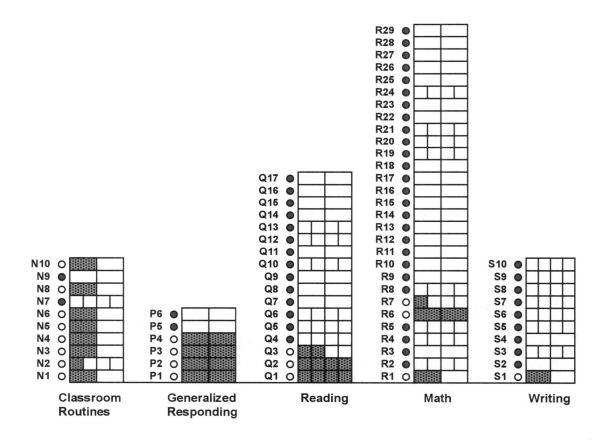

Advanced Learner Assessment Sections N-S

Classroom Routines

Generalized Responding

Reading

Math

Writing

M. Group Instruction

Jason is able to use his existing skills and to learn some new skills in a small group instruction (1 teacher to 3 students) (M12=2). He will take turns and provide answers to questions he knows (M11=2). However, when the group size is increased to 4 or more students, his level of attention and participation decreases considerably (M1=3, M2=0).

N. Classroom Routines

Jason is able to follow most classroom routines such as putting away his materials (N8=1) and hanging up his backpack upon arrival at school, but he frequently requires prompts to complete these tasks (N1=1).

P. Generalized Responding

The skills that Jason acquires readily generalize to novel stimuli (P1=2), and he uses his skills with a variety of individuals (P2=2) in all environments (P3=2). However, he uses his skills as they were taught and does not spontaneously vary his responding (P5=0).

Academic Skills Section

Q. Reading

Jason can both receptively identify and label the letters of the alphabet (Q1&2=4). He can select 5 letters when given the sounds associated with the letters (Q3=2), but he cannot make the sounds of those letters when shown those letters (Q4=0). Jason cannot read any words (Q10=0) and is unable to match any words to pictures (Q5=0).

R. Math

Jason is able to label the numbers 1 to 10 (R7=1), is able to rote count to 8 (R2=0), and is able to count out 3 items (R4=0).

Advanced Learner Assessment Sections T-X

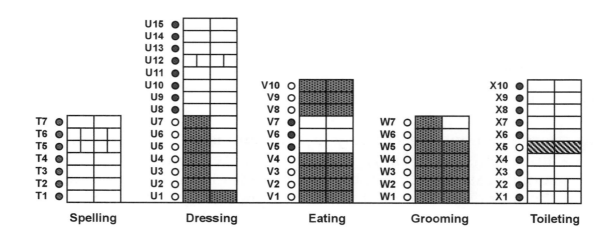

S. Writing

Jason is able to mark on paper when a crayon and paper are given to him (S1=1), but he is unable to color within boundaries (S2=0). He is unable to trace simple straight and curved lines accurately (S3=0).

T. Spelling

Jason is unable to spell (All T=0).

Self-Help Skills Section

U. Dressing Skills

Jason can pull up and down his pants for toileting (U1=2), and he can remove his shoes, socks, and shirt (U2-7=1). He is unable to put on his clothing independently and is unable to close zippers and fasten buttons (U11-14=0).

V. Eating Skills

Jason uses utensils to eat (V4=2) and drinks from a cup without spilling (V3=2). He keeps his eating area clean and throws his trash away after meals (V9&10=2).

W. Grooming

Jason is able to independently wash and dry his hands and face (W1-4=2). He requires prompts to brush his teeth and to use a tissue to blow his nose (W6&7=1).

X. Toileting

Jason wears diapers and has never eliminated in a toilet. He does ask to have his diaper changed when it is wet (All X=0).

Advanced Learner Assessment Sections Y-Z

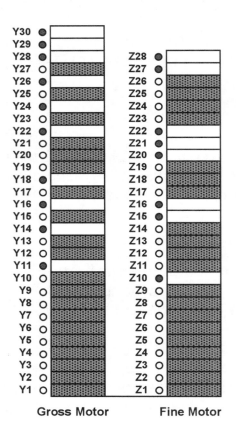

Gross Motor   Fine Motor

Motor Skills Section

Y. Gross Motor Skills

Jason can walk forwards and backwards (Y1&7=1) and can hop (Y8=1) and throw/catch a ball (Y9&15=1). He is uninterested in riding a tricycle (Y16=0) and has difficulty with motor activities that require reciprocal motion (Y11&29=0).

Z. Fine Motor Skills

Jason can do a variety of fine motor activities such as simple single-piece inset puzzles (Z3=1), stack blocks (Z13=1), string beads (Z14=1), and mark on paper with a crayon (Z1=1). He has difficulty removing lids from jars (Z15=0), using a pencil accurately (Z10, 20 &28=0), and cutting (Z16&27=0).

Educational Priorities for Jason

In a review of the Basic Learner Skills Section, there are several major educational priorities that need to be addressed for Jason. These priorities include teaching him several important language skills (i.e., advanced requesting and labeling skills, and intraverbal skills), teaching him to wait to receive a reinforcer, and increasing his ability to remain on-task in a small group instructional format.

Although Jason can receptively identify and label over 150 items and knows some verbs, his language skills are still quite limited. His ability to label actions and use adjectives, pronouns and prepositions should continue to be developed. Jason has difficulty in talking about items that are not present. He needs to acquire skills in asking for items that are not present and asking for information. Although he now understands many of the instructions that are given to him and can ask others for some items that are important to him, he still lacks skills in getting his needs met whenever items are not within his sight. When he wants an item that is not present or needs an item that is missing to complete a task, he does not know how to ask who has an item or where an item is located. Thus, a critical skill that he must acquire is his ability to request these types of information.

Jason's intraverbal skills are quite weak. His social interactions with others are limited by his inability to talk about items. Although he frequently attempts to interact with others, his limited intraverbal skills do not allow for extended interactions with peers. He needs to develop skills in talking about items and activities, without being dependent upon having those items or activities being present. Interventions to strengthen this repertoire can utilize his strong receptive language skills by using procedures to teach receptive by function, feature, and class skills, and then transferring the receptive skills to intraverbal skills (Sundberg & Partington, 1998).

Jason's inability to wait for the delivery of a reinforcer poses several problems for further development of his skills. Whenever a reinforcer is not readily forthcoming, he will either go off-task or engage in disruptive behavior. Thus, he is able to be instructed only in a very small group of students by individuals who are trained to pay careful attention to his reinforcement schedule. To be able to acquire new skills in groups of typically developing peers (who provide numerous models of appropriate language and social interaction skills), he will need to participate in tasks with a leaner schedule of reinforcement.

An IEP has been developed for Jason based upon the review of his skills provided by *The ABLLS™-R* (See Appendix 3). Specific learning objectives were identified for Jason (see objectives listed below). Objectives were included in several of the skill areas in *The ABLLS™-R*; primarily from the Basic Learner Skills section of the assessment.

There are several objectives to increase his visual performance skills (Objectives 1, 2, & 3). It is important that he continue to develop his skills that require him to attend to visual stimuli. Learning to attend to more subtle details of the stimuli is important for Jason to be able to develop more complex verbal skills, especially those skills related to the properties of items (e.g., adjectives) and the relationships between items (e.g., prepositions).

"Advanced Learner" Objectives

1. When given a model of a visual pattern, Jason will be able to make a block design that matches a picture using up to 5 blocks when given more blocks than are necessary to complete the task.

2. Jason will be able to put together a variety of eight-piece (or more) puzzles without frames.

3. When given a sample sequence pattern consisting of items, Jason will arrange additional items to extend the pattern following the original sequence.

4. Jason will be able to go independently to any known person and request a specified object and bring back the object.

(Continued on page 70)

"Advanced Learner" Objectives (continued)

5. Jason will be able to receptively identify and label (i.e., tact) a total of at least 10 prepositions.

6. Jason will be able to receptively identify and label (i.e., tact) at least 6 pronouns.

7. Jason will be able to select a specified item that has two specified characteristics (i.e., "The big red ball").

8. Jason will be able to select 1 item from a display of 3 items when told one of the item's features, function, or class for 2 aspects of at least 50 of his known items (e.g., "Touch the one you eat").

9. Jason will imitate a gross motor activity matching the speed of a model.

10. Jason will be able to imitate a sequence of motor activities without additional prompts (i.e., "Clap hands, tap thighs, then tap table").

11. Jason will be able to ask for information using "who" and "where" questions.

12. Jason will be able to request (i.e., mand) any known item needed to complete a task.

13. Jason will label (i.e., tact) 20 common actions (both on going and pictures).

14. When given a visual display (pictures or items), Jason will be able to label at least 50 items when told their function, feature, or class.

15. Jason will be able to receptively identify and label (i.e., tact) items using adjectives, for at least 15 non-color adjectives (e.g., big/little).

(Continued on page 72)

Although Jason's receptive language skills are relatively strong compared to his other language skills, it is also important to continue developing these skills. Therefore, there are several objectives to further develop his receptive identification of prepositions (Objective 5), pronouns (Objective 6), and his ability to discriminate items given multiple criteria (e.g., the big red ball) (Objective 7). He also needs to learn to follow directions to go to others and request a specified item (Objective 4). Another receptive skill that is included is that of teaching Jason to identify items when told something about the item, but not directly given the item's name (e.g., the one you eat) (Objective 8). As mentioned previously, the ability to receptively identify an item when told either its function, feature, or class to which the item belongs can be an important skill that facilitates the development of the child's intraverbal skills.

There are two objectives included to improve Jason's imitation skills. Although he can readily imitate a variety of actions, he still needs to learn to imitate sequences of actions (Objective 10) and to imitate movements that match the speed of modeled action (Objective 9). There are numerous social activities that require not only a specified movement, but also require that the movement be completed at a certain rate (e.g., twirling an end of a jump rope, singing a song at the same rate as the others in a group).

There are several verbal skill areas that Jason needs to develop. As mentioned previously, Jason needs to learn to ask for information and for items that are not present. He has recently started to ask "what" questions to obtain the names of items, but he does not ask for other types of information. Therefore, there are objectives included to teach him to ask "who" and "where" questions (Objective 11) and to ask for missing items needed to complete a task (Objective 12). Objectives were included to increase his ability to label actions (Objective 13) and adjectives (Objective 15). An objective was also included to increase his skills in labeling items when shown a display of items and given some information about one of the items (Objective 14).

Jason's weakest verbal skills are in the intraverbal section. It is extremely important for him to develop his ability to talk about items and activities that are not present. Therefore, there are

"Advanced Learner" Objectives (continued)

16. Jason will correctly respond to 25 intraverbal fill ins (e.g., "Barney is a _____," "When your hair is messy, you need a _____," etc.).

17. Jason will be able to verbally name members of specific categories.

18. Jason will be able to provide answers to 4 questions regarding personal information (i.e., first and last name, age, and phone number).

19. Jason will play with toys while engaging in multiple responses consistent with an identifiable theme, for at least 5 activities or 5 toys.

20. Jason will participate in sociodramatic play activities in which he pretends to be at least 5 different characters (e.g., chef, doctor, conductor).

21. Jason will initiate and return greetings with peers without prompting.

22. Jason will follow instructions that are known by him (e.g., touch known items, imitate an action, etc.) that are presented to a group of four students.

23. Jason will appropriately take turns with three other students during group instruction activities.

24. Jason will be able to label (i.e., tact) the sounds of 15 letters.

25. Jason will be able to match at least 10 words to their corresponding picture.

26. Jason will be able to match a numeral to the same number of items given to him for up to 20 items.

27. Jason will be able to label (i.e., tact) the numerals 1 to 31.

(Continued on page 74)

several objectives to develop his skills in this area. Objectives are included that address his ability to fill in words of a phrase (e.g., you sleep in a _____) (Objective 16), name members of a specified category (e.g., name some things you eat) (Objective 17), and to provide answers to questions regarding personal information (e.g., name, phone number) (Objective 18).

There are several additional objectives included in his IEP to address basic learner skills in the areas of play and social interaction. These objectives include increasing the variety of play actions while manipulating toys (Objective 19), pretend play activities (Objective 20), and initiating and returning greetings to peers (Objective 21). Increasing his play skills and his initiations of interactions with peers makes it more likely that he will be able to have greater opportunities to interact with and learn from his peers.

Although there are no specific objectives included from the cooperation and reinforcer effectiveness section, his ability to work when his schedule of reinforcement is thinned should be addressed by his educational staff. There are two objectives to improve his group participation skills in a group size that is slightly larger than groups in which he is already successfully participating (i.e., 1:4 vs. 1:3) (Objectives 22 & 23). By developing his skills within a larger group, his reinforcement schedule can be gradually thinned by a teacher who is a skillful behavior shaper. His IEP also includes an objective to reduce his instances of disruptive behavior, which has been demonstrated to be a result of his schedule of reinforcement (Objective 34).

There are several other areas of the basic learner skills that were not included in the set of educational objectives. There were no objectives to develop his vocal imitation skills, spontaneous vocalizations, or generalized responding because his skills in these areas were already fairly strong in comparison to his other skill areas. Even though he has relatively weak skills in following classroom routines and in his use of syntax and grammar, these skill areas were not selected as areas of priority at this time. The classroom routines are somewhat developed and should continue to develop without requiring elaborately designed procedures, but merely through the simple fading of prompts by instructional staff. The syntax and grammar skills will take more careful shaping.

Advanced Learner Objectives (continued)

28. Jason will be able to count out objects from a larger set for at least 20 objects.

29. Jason will be able to rote count to the number 20 without prompts.

30. Jason will be able to trace simple straight and curved lines, and shapes, staying within 1/4 inch of the model.

31. Jason will be able to color within lined areas without prompts.

32. Jason will urinate in the toilet at least 2 times a day.

33. Jason will be able to cut out simple shapes staying within 1/4 inch of the line.

34. Jason will reduce instances of hitting staff and throwing materials to 50% of baseline levels.

However, his limited language skills are already following correct formal patterns. As he is taught more advanced labeling and intraverbal skills, there is every reason to believe that these language conventions will continue to be acquired through the modeling and reinforcement provided during the acquisition process. Once the more pragmatic aspects of his language skills are developed (e.g., advanced requesting and labeling skills, intraverbal skills), it will be necessary to review for specific deficits in the formal aspects of his language skills.

Because Jason has begun to develop some basic academic skills, several objectives were included to improve his abilities in the areas of reading, math and writing. He can already label the letters of the alphabet and can receptively identify some letters when given their corresponding sounds. Therefore, there are objectives to teach him to provide the sounds of some letters (Objective 24) and to match words to pictures (Objective 25). In the math area, there are several objectives to extend his skills in labeling numbers (Objective 27), rote counting (Objective 29), counting objects from a larger set (Objective 28), and matching a numeral to a set of objects (Objective 26). In the writing area, there are objectives to help focus on his fine motor skills of coloring within boundaries (Objective 31) and tracing simple lines (Objective 30).

There are two remaining objectives included to address his self-help skills and his motor skills. Although he could work on numerous self-help skills (especially in the area of dressing) many of these skills can be addressed through the course of daily events in his home environment. However, because he is five years old and is still not toilet trained, this particular deficit should be addressed in both the home and school environments (Objective 32). With the exception of coordination-related motor skills, his skills in these areas are quite well developed. However, an objective to increase his ability to use scissors was included to help develop some of his fine motor coordination (Objective 33).

Appendix 1: Information Regarding the Revision of The ABLLS™-R Protocol

The original *ABLLS™-R Protocol* and *ABLLS™-R Guide* were first published in 1998. Since that time, it has proven to be a useful tool for assisting parents and professionals to identify skills from a variety of repertoires that are associated with students' developmental delays. Once specific skill deficits have been identified, it is then possible to provide instruction to help teach those skills to the student and track the skill development within the various repertoires. Although research is still needed to help us identify the most critical skills that a child needs to acquire to learn from his everyday interactions and the most effective intervention strategies, it is evident that systematic and intensive instruction of basic skills results in individuals who are better able to learn new skills as they interact with others in a variety of settings.

As professionals continue to work with children, they acquire additional information regarding intervention strategies both through peer-reviewed research projects and through the implementation of intervention services. As a result, there have been several areas of investigation that have influenced how parents and practitioners attempt to help students develop a variety of skills. Some of the significant areas of investigation include an analysis of motivational variables affecting a learner, a more comprehensive analysis of social interaction, imitation, and intraverbal language skills, the investigation of a learner's ability to fluently use his existing skills, an analysis of shared or joint attention, and an analysis of learner readiness skills.

Major Areas of Conceptual and Methodological Investigation

Motivation

Although it has been the goal of many parents and professionals to be able to help children transition from receiving reinforcement from frequent powerful reinforcers to more infrequently delivered socially oriented types of reinforcers, the development of these socially-oriented reinforcers has proven to be difficult for many individuals.

Social Skills Development

The development of effective social interaction skills has been area of concern for many individuals with developmental disabilities. The recent focus of specific interventions to develop these skills has helped with the identification of many of the subtle skills that are needed by individuals to be able to interact with and learn from their peers. Many of these skills have been added to the revised version of the ABLLS™-R.

Fluency

One of the major research areas with regard to skill development has been related to the concern that students often acquire basic skills but lack the ability to quickly use them when they are required in a variety of contexts (e.g., learning more complex skills that require the basic skills, using the skills during everyday activities). Therefore, the revised version of the ABLLS™-R Protocol includes scoring criteria to help ensure that children are capable of using their acquired skills in a fluent manner.

Imitation

The importance of having a well-developed imitative repertoire has been recognized by parents and professionals as critical to development of a wide variety of language, self-help, motor, academic and social skills. The updated version of the ABLLS™-R Protocol has incorporated many new skill items that help to extend the parent's and professional's ability to determine the extent of a child's ability to attend to the subtle features of the actions of others and to the ability to replicate those actions. Many of the new skills have been included to ensure both greater amount of time attending to the behaviors being modeled by others and to the ability to recall those actions following the demonstrated actions.

Intraverbal

As researchers attempt to teach children how to converse about a wide variety of topics, much has been learned about the many skills required of a child to listen to the words of others and to be able to provide verbal responses related to the topic being addressed in the conversation. The current version includes many new distinctions of skills that attempt to more clearly identify these skills and situations in which a child might use those skills.

Joint Attention

Another area of considerable research has been related to the ability of children to share attention with others to items and events that occur in the presence of both individuals. This ability to see that others are also observing a similar item or event is a skill that is critical for the development of more advanced social interactions. As a result, several new items have been added to the current version to help with the tracking and development of this important skill area.

Learner Readiness

One of the major factors that influences a student's ability to acquire new skills is his willingness to follow the directions from those who are attempting to teach him. Therefore, the task of the instructor is considerably easier when the student is able to follow a sequence of directions for intermittent social reinforcers than when the student requires frequent powerful reinforcers in order to follow very simple directions. The current version of the ABLLS™-R has incorporated several new items to measure the student's ability to work both with a variety of individuals and to do so while attending to the reinforcing feedback of a social nature.

Additionally, many educational tasks require the presentation of materials in a display that can best be presented on a table. Therefore, it is critical that children learn a variety of skills related to the participation with an instructor who has placed the material in front of the student. Specifically, the child needs to be able to focus on the materials, attend to the instructions being provided to him and then follow through with the requested actions in a timely manner.

Length of Attention to Tasks

In order to acquire many important skills, it is necessary for a student to be able to have focused attention to a set of steps involved in the task. The development of an adequate attention span is assessed in several new items that have been included in the current version of the ABLLS™-R.

Addition of New Tasks to the Skill Sequences

Information obtained from several of major conceptual areas has been incorporated in the current revision of the ABLLS™-R Protocol. Many of these concepts have been incorporated into new items included in the current list of skills and into the scoring criteria associated with previously included items.

Samples of Skill Acquisition Used in the Readjustment of the Skill Sequences

The adjustment of the sequencing of skills was based on ABLLS™-R scores from both children with developmental delays and typically developing children. There were a total of 30 protocols reviewed, 24 were completed for students with developmental delays and 6 for children with typical development. Individuals who were trained to complete the ABLLS™-R had scored each of the protocols. The children with developmental delays ranged in age from 2 years, 2 months of age through 7 years, 9 months of age, with a mean age of 4 years, 4 months. Three of the children with developmental delays were females and 21 were males. The children with typical development ranged in age from 3 years, 1 month to 5 years, 0 months of age, with a mean age of 4 years, 1 month. The sample of typically developing children included a male and a female at approximately the ages of 3 years, 1 month, 4 years, 0 months, and 5 years, 0 months.

Important Implications of Developing Teaching Strategies When Using the Skill Sequences

The addition of new skills into the original sequence of items was completed at the same time as the readjustment of the original sequences. The positioning of the new skill items was arranged based on the apparent level of difficulty in relation to the level of difficulty of the original items. Additional data regarding the sequences that include new items will need to be reviewed in the future. The addition and deletion of items and the adjustment of the sequence of items is a continuous process.

Because of the unique learning histories of students with developmental delays, it is not possible to determine an exact level of task difficulty and develop an exact sequence of skill acquisition for any skill repertoire area. It must be remembered that the skills in each sequence are related to skills in other repertoires areas; a skill acquired in one area (e.g., receptive language) may make it possible to acquire a skill in a different area (e.g., labeling or intraverbal). The selection of skills to be taught to a student must be done on an individual basis. As such, it is important for individuals who are developing educational programs for specific students to select skills to be taught based upon the student's readiness to learn each skill, rather than merely selecting a skill because it is a lower task item than some items that have been acquired by the student, or because it is the next item in the sequence that has not yet been acquired.

The *ABLLS™-R Protocol* does not specify what skills should be taught to a particular child at a specific point in the student's development. Decisions regarding the selection of goals, objectives and learning tasks should be made with the input of planning teams involving parents and trained professionals.

Analysis of Changes in Specific Skill Areas

There were substantive changes made in 18 of the 25 sections in the ABLLS™-R Protocol. There were only minor changes made to the scoring criteria for one task in four sections (i.e., Section I. Spontaneous Vocalizations, U. Dressing Skills, Section V. Eating Skills, and Section X. Toileting Skills). No changes were made in three sections (i.e., Sections J. Syntax and Grammar, P. Generalization, and W. Grooming Skills).

For each section of the ABLLS™-R Protocol that has had significant changes, the modifications are described in a narrative format along with tables to highlight the differences from the original version and the revised version. The substantive changes included modification of the scoring criteria for items, the inclusion of new task items, and a reordering of the sequencing for some of the items included in the previous version. Additionally, some changes in the wording of the task objectives, questions to ascertain skill levels, and examples were made to make it easier for assessors to clarify the intent of the task items.

A summary of the substantive changes in 18 sections is provided below. It should be noted that the tables are arranged according to the revised sequence of skills. The original task numbers are listed to the left of the new task number so that individuals who have used the earlier version of the ABLLS™-R Protocol can easily make a comparison between the previous and current versions. Indications of the nature of the changes (e.g., change in criteria, change in examples, inclusion of a new item) are specified to the right of each modified or new task item (shown in bold). A highlighting (i.e., bold) of the original task item number indicates those original tasks that were moved to an earlier location in the sequence.

Description of the Revisions by Section

A. Cooperation and Reinforcer Effectiveness:

A total of eight new skills were added to this section that measures the student's cooperation with others who are attempting to teach him new skills. One of the new skills (A5) includes the tendency of the student to approach an instructor who has a clearly identified reinforcer even when the student knows from past experience, in this type of situation, that he will need to make a simple required response before obtaining the reinforcer from the instructor. Another new item (A7) measures the student's ability to work for a variety of instructors. Some children have demonstrated being able to work well with only one or two instructors. The ability to learn from a variety of individuals increases the student's options for acquiring skills in a variety of circumstances.

Several new items are related to a student's ability to participate in learning activities that involve the presentation of materials at a table. These items include waiting for an instruction without handling the materials (A8), looking to the instructor to determine what he is to do with the materials (A9), scanning the materials prior to responding to an instruction (A10), and responding quickly once an instruction is given (A11).

Several new items are included that seek to measure the student's tendency to be reinforced by social interaction with the instructor. New items include a measure as to whether interactions with the instructor serve as reinforcers (A14) and whether the student attends to changes in the instructor's voice and facial expression when the instructor praises correct responses (A15).

The skill involving the student waiting when a reinforcer is delayed (old A11) has been moved to precede seeking approval following task completion items (old A9) and the completion of a task serving as a reinforcer (old A10). This change was based upon samples of student scores that indicated that this skill often precedes the development of other skills.

Finally, the criteria for several items were modified to allow for more precision in the evaluation of the skills. The criteria for tasks A1-A4 now include a specific amount of time in which the student must respond in order to receive credit for those skills (e.g., responds within 3 seconds).

B. Visual Performance

Six new items were added to this section that measure the student's ability to attend to visual stimuli. Four new items include skills that correspond to those in which the same concept was included in other skill repertoire areas of the ABLLS™-R (e.g., Receptive Language, Labeling, Intraverbal) that was previously not part of this section. These items include the ability to match associated pictures (B16) and sort items based on their function, features, or membership within a class (B17 – B 19). In addition, a new item to measure the ability to engage in fluent matching (B7) and yet another to measure the student's ability to match items to a different one attending to when those objects are placed by another person (B24).

Several items from the previous version of the ABLLS™-R were moved to a different location in the skill sequence based upon data that indicated that the skills were frequently observed to be acquired earlier or later in the learning sequence. The skill of inserting single inset puzzle pieces (old B10) was moved to the start of the sequence (B1) and inserting pieces into a form box (old B9) was moved to follow the inset puzzle item (B2). Additionally, the ability to match objects to pictures (old B4) was moved to earlier in the sequence because it was often acquired prior to the skills of matching pictures to pictures (old B2) and before matching pictures to objects (old B3). Similarly, the ability to complete puzzles in an inset frame (old B11) and completing puzzles with a square-edged frame (old B12) were moved to earlier in the sequence because these skills were observed to be acquired prior to the skill of doing block designs from a picture (old B7).

C. Receptive Language

Numerous changes have been made to this skill repertoire area. The changes are based on both the data from the acquisition of learner skills and observations of skills that are required of students in a variety of tasks (e.g., educational, social, and daily living). These changes include the addition of new skills, changing the criteria for several items, and a reordering of several skills.

Six new skill items were added to this repertoire area and one item from the previous version was deleted. The previous item of looking at a common object (old C4) was deleted because it was observed that this skill was redundant in that it usually was obtained at the same time as the skill of looking at reinforcing items (old C3) and this skill was also incorporated in the task of touching common items in a variety of positions (old C6). Several new items were included to measure the concepts that correspond to the same concept measured in other skill repertoire areas. These items include the touching of parts of items (C23) and selecting all of the examples of an item (C46). Additionally, new items were included to measure the fluency of receptive responses (C19), to measure the ability to follow another person's gaze (C25) to select items, to follow a person's hand signals (C26), and the ability to perform multiple actions with objects (C33).

There were changes made to numerous items such as to allow for more accurate determination of the skill levels. For example, several items that had criteria of "readily looks" or "readily finds" have now been changed to more specific measures (e.g., "within 3 seconds," "80% of the time").

Several items in the previous Receptive Language section (following the old C15) were reordered based upon student data regarding the acquisition of skills. For example, the ability to select items given a variety of instructions (not discrimination of the instructions) (old C 16) was moved to later in the skill sequence. Similarly, the ability to select objects (old C23) and pictures from an array of three (now six) samples (old C24), the measure of the rate of acquisition of new receptive items (old C35) and the ability to select associated pictures (old C44) were moved to earlier in the sequence of skills. The skills involving the receptive identification of items based on their functions (old C20), features (old C21), and class (old C22), have been moved to later in the sequence, as have the items regarding the selection of "same" and "different" (old C46) and the selection of "non-examples" (old C49).

D. Imitation

There has been a major increase in the number of imitation skills included in this repertoire area that requires the student to attend to visual stimuli produced by the actions of others and then match the actions. The increase has more than doubled the number of items from 13 to 27 items. Many of the new items involve the student attending for longer periods of time to more complex sequences actions and attend to the dynamic properties of the modeled action.

There are several new items that measure whether the student can match the dynamic characteristics of the model. The ability to attend to how an action is performed includes items that assess whether the student can make both static and kinetic types of imitative responses (D6), the ability to match the speed of both an ongoing model (D15) and following a model (D16), the ability to match the intensity of an action (D21), and the number of times a specific action is performed (D22). Additionally, the ability to respond imitatively when provided with varied statements indicating the need to imitate an action (D7) has been included in the revised set of skills.

New items have been included to ensure that students are able to match a sequence of modeled responses. For example, new items include the ability to touch items in sequence along with a model (D13), and in a sequence following a model (D18). Additionally, the ability to imitate a sequence of actions involving multiple items (D24) has now been included.

Several items have been included to ensure that the student has mastery of imitative skills that facilitate the development of other critical vocal skills and group participation skills. The ability to observe and imitate modeled gross motor response in a mirror (D8) and imitation of facial movements in a mirror (D11), as well as imitation of a blowing action (D13) has been added. Additional items also include the ability to fluently switch between actions following the lead of a model (D19) and imitation of simultaneous motor and vocal responses (D23).

Finally, there was a change in the previous sequence of items based on data from student performance. These observations resulted in placing the acquisition of fine motor response (old D9) prior to the ability to match the speed of an action (old D8).

E. Vocal Imitation

There was a significant increase in the number of new skill items added to this section that involves a student's ability to imitate a vocal model. A greater emphasis has been placed on focusing on the ability to attend and fluently produce a wide variety of sound patterns and combinations that are prerequisites to the imitation of words and sentences.

Several new items focus on the student attending to how simple sounds are produced. The ability to fluently make simple sounds (E2), to make multiple separate sound combinations (E4), to imitate sounds both quickly and slowly (E5), and to imitate the number of repetitions of a sound (E6) have been included.

New items have also been included to track the development of the ability to make specific sound combinations. For example, there is a difference between making the individual sounds (e.g., "mm" and "ee") and making a combination of the sounds (e.g., "me"). The second example requires a fluent transition from one sound to the next. A new item assesses the ability to hold a sound and transition to a new sound (E7), and skills involving specific consonant and vowel combinations are now tracked in several items (E8, E9, & E10).

Observations of student variation in ability to attend to specific types of variations in the dynamic characteristics of vocal models (i.e., prosody), has resulted in a separation of those skills. Specifically, the original prosody item (old E7) has now been split into three skill items: the ability to repeat sounds fast and slowly (E5), repeat words fast and slowly (E15), repeat sounds and words loudly and softly (E16), and repeat sounds and words in a high- and low-pitched voice (E 17).

Although repeating a message is often considered a social interaction skill, the ability to deliver a message to another person requires the both ability to vocally imitate and to remember what was said to him. Therefore, a new task item has been added to ensure that vocal imitation skills can be utilized when delivering a message to others (E18).

F. Requesting

There have been only a few changes made to this section that measures the ability to request items, actions and information.

There have been two additional items included in this set of skills, but the sequencing of several of the items has been changed to correspond with data from observations of student skill acquisition.

The new items involve the student's ability to request items when they are not within sight (F6) and to look at a person when he is requesting items (F7). It is important for students to be able to ask for items they cannot see and it is important for the student to look at the individual to whom they are requesting items, actions and/or information.

Data regarding the sequence of acquisition of the skills in this section required only minimal changes. Several items in the previous Requesting section (mainly following the old F11) were reordered based upon student data regarding the acquisition of skills. The item involving requests for attention (old F7) was moved to later in the sequence, and the items involving the rate of acquisition (old F 26), using adjectives to request (old F 22), prepositions (old F 23), future events and items (old F 21), adverbs (old F 24), and pronouns (old F 25) were moved to earlier positions in the sequence.

G. Labeling

Several changes have been made to the labeling skill repertoire area. The changes are based on both the data from the acquisition of learner skills and observations of skills that are required of students in a variety of tasks (e.g., educational, social, and daily living). These changes include the addition of five new skills (including concepts that correspond to the same concept measured in other skill repertoire areas), a reordering of several skills, and some changes in the criteria to measure several skills.

Several new items were added to this list of skills. The new skills include the ability to label clothing (G6), to fluently label known items (G9), to label associated pictures (G14), to label specific aspects of an item (G26), and to label items at a distance (G32).

Several items in the previous Labeling section (following the old G8) were reordered based upon student data regarding the acquisition of skills. The ability to label body parts (old G9) and the skill of labeling items with a "yes" or "no" response (old G18) were moved to an earlier position in the sequence. Additionally, several two-component labels' tasks were moved to an earlier position in the sequence including the two-component labeling of: two nouns using objects (old G22), using pictures (old G23), using a carrier phrase (old G24), noun and verb (old G25), and noun and adjective (old G26). Three-component labeling (old G34 and G35) were moved to a later position in the sequence of skills.

H. Intraverbal

Numerous changes have been made to the intraverbal repertoire area. The changes are based on both the data from the acquisition of learner skills and observations of skills that are required of students in a variety of tasks (e.g., educational, social, and daily living). These changes include the addition of new skills, the separation of previous skill items into several new skills (to allow a more precise determination of previously included skills), changing the criteria for several items, and a reordering of several skills.

The ability to attend to the words of others and give a different verbal response when talking about items, events and individuals is a difficult task for many students with developmental delays. It is necessary for a student to not merely give rote responses to questions, but to be able to listen to the questions and comments of others and be able to make an appropriate verbal response given the specifics of what was said to him. He must be able to determine if he is being asked to discuss what happened, where an event occurs, who was involved, etc. It is also important for the student to be able to talk about a wide variety of topics concerning his daily activities, as well as his home, school and community.

Several previously included items have been separated into a few new items to allow for a more precise measure of a student's ability to answer questions and talk about a wide variety of topics concerning his daily activities, as well as his home, school and community. The skill of answering "What" questions (old H16) has now been separated into the skills of answering these types of questions about items in the home (H10), regarding the functions of items (H11), and regarding items and activities in the community (H23 & H24). Similarly, "Where" questions (old H 17) have been separated into skills regarding the home (H12), activities in the home (H13) and items and activities in the community (H25). The skill of naming items previously observed (old H 18) has now been split into three items involving previously observed items (H19), activities (H20) and people (H21).

Four new skill items were added to this repertoire area and four items from the previous version were deleted. The task of providing "opposites" (e.g., hot-cold) when given a verbal stimulus (old H15) was eliminated due to the rote nature of the responses. The previous task of answering questions regarding community resources and activities (old H33) was eliminated because these same skills are now measured in a more specific manner in several new tasks (H23 - H25). The previous items of answering questions regarding academic material (old H37 & H38) were deleted because it was observed that these items were not easy to define because of the extreme diversity of what might be considered "academic." Several new items were included to measure concepts that correspond to the same ones measured in other skill repertoire areas. These items include providing intraverbal associations (H7), discriminating specific questions about items, activities and individuals (H30), and describing items (H41). One final item was added regarding the use of intraverbal skills in classroom discussions (H48).

Several items have slightly modified descriptions, examples, or criteria. For example, the criteria item pertaining to maintaining a conversation (H44) has been changed to require the student to ask a question or make a novel comment during the interaction. The task objective for the item involving stating the name of an item given a description of the item (old H27) and the example and criteria were changed for the item regarding telling a story (old H42) to include telling about experiences.

The sequencing of several items was changed based upon data indicating that the skills were often observed to be acquired earlier or later than some of the other skills in the sequence. For example, the skills of filling in an item given the class of the item (old H12), providing multiple responses given a category (old H13), making related comments (old H24), maintaining a conversation (old H39), answering novel questions (old H40) and providing multiple responses regarding the community (old H34) were moved to earlier positions in sequence. Additionally, the skills of answering "Which" questions (old H20) and spontaneously making comments in conversations (old H41) were moved to later in the sequence.

K. Play & Leisure Skills

A relatively small number of changes have been made to the play and leisure skill repertoire area. The changes are based on both the data from the acquisition of learner skills and observations of skills that are required of students in play and leisure activities. These changes include the addition of new skills, the separation of previous skill items into several new skills, changing the criteria for several items, and a reordering of several skills.

Five new skills were added to the play and leisure skills section. These items include allowing others to touch the toys they are using (K2), playing with a variety of peers (K9), playing simple games with balls (K12), coordinated play with peers (following instructions from peers) (K13), and participating in interactive motor games (K14).

Several of the previous skill items were altered to allow a more precise determination of those skills. For example, the previous item of outdoor games and activities (old K10) was separated into independent outdoor activities (K3) and interactive motor games (K14). The interactive play with peers (old K5) was changed such that it eliminated allowing others to be near them from the criteria for measuring the skill. The previous item related to appropriate interactive leisure activities (old K9) was changed to a measure of the ability to play board games (K15), and the skill of playing dress-up was incorporated into the socio-dramatic play item (K10).

The sequencing of several items in this section was changed based upon data indicating that the skills were often observed to be acquired earlier or later than some of the other skills in the sequence. Specifically, independent play with toys and engages in verbal behavior (old K4), socio-dramatic play (old K7), indoor leisure activities (old K 8) and independent outdoor activities (old K10) were moved to earlier positions in the sequnce of skills.

L. Social Interactions

A significant number of new skill items have been added to the social interaction section. Both researchers and practitioners have given a considerable amount of attention in the last few years to the specific behaviors involved in the development of social interaction skills. Some of these skills involve the careful observation of the behavior of others, while other skills require the development of advanced language skills.

Thirteen new skill items were added to this repertoire area. The additional skills include looking at others in anticipation of a reinforcing event (L7), searching for a missing person (L14), active appropriate attention seeking (L15), joining peers in an activity (L22), observation of peer's attention to activities (L23), responding to feedback from peers (L24), adjusting behavior based on the actions of peers (L25), assisting others to participate (L26), stating items and activities others like or dislike (L27), directing others to items of interest to that person (L28), attending to the reactions of interest to items and activities by others (L29), delivering a message (L30), and waiting for a break to enter a conversation (L31).

There have been changes made to the criterion or examples of a few previously included items. For example, the criteria for taking offered items (old L7) has been changed, the behavior expected to be observed when tolerating interactions with others (old L2), and examples have been added regarding the showing an interest in the behavior of others (old L3). The skill of accepting offers to join an activity (old L8) was deleted because that skill was included in another task item (old L4). Finally, the task name and criteria for maintaining (now obtaining and maintaining) the attention of others (old L22) have been changed.

M. Group Instruction

There were only a few minor changes made to the group instruction section. These changes included adding examples related to appropriate behavior in a group situation (M1 & M2), changing the location of the tasks and the criteria for responding at the same time as other students (M5 & M6), and a change in the description of the objective of raising a hand to participate in an activity (M7).

N. Following Classroom Routines

There were several changes in the sequencing of tasks in the section pertaining to following classroom routines. The change in sequencing was based upon data from students' acquisition of the various skills. Specifically, following classroom routines (old N10), working independently on non-academic tasks (old N4) and academic tasks (old N5), remaining seated during transitions (old N7), physically transitioning between activities (old N6), and waiting for a turn to do an activity (old N9) were moved to earlier positions in the sequence of skills.

Q. Reading Skills

There were only a few minor changes in the Reading Skills section. Two new items were included regarding the skills of being able to read a passage and perform an action (Q 15), and follow directions related to worksheet tasks (Q16). The criteria for the ability to decode words (Q11) were changed to ensure the student could use this skill with unknown words. Finally the skill of answering reading comprehension was changed to Q17.

R. Math Skills

There were numerous changed made in the Math Skills section. Many of the changes were from the data obtained on the acquisition of these skills by typically developing children. Several of the items in the previous sequence were adjusted based on the observations of student acquisition of the skills. The major changes in the sequence involves moving the concepts of "more," "less," "some," "all," and "none" to an earlier portion of the sequence. Additionally, time telling skills (old R11), skills involving coins (R12-14), and skills involving adding items to a specified quantity (old R9) and adding numbers (old R10) were moved to later in the sequence of skills.

In addition to changes to several items in the math skills sequence, there were three tasks for which the scoring criteria were modified. These items included counting objects with prompts (R3), counting a given set of objects (R4), and use of coins (R24). The one new skill that was added to the math skills section involves the functional skill of being able to go a short distance to get a specified number of items (R19). This skill was added to ensure the generalized use of basic counting skills in tasks that may occur in many daily activities.

One of the major changes included the combination of the expressive labeling and receptive discrimination of many of the language concepts used in math related tasks (old R15-42). This change was made because it was observed that when children have the ability to do math related tasks, their language skills are usually such that when they acquire the math concepts, they acquire the ability to receptively identify and label these concepts at about the same time. Therefore, tracking these skills within the same task item results in greater efficiency when scoring these items.

S. Writing Skills

There was only one change to the Writing Skills section. This change was the separation of the skills of tracing lines, shapes, numbers and letters (old S3) into two skill items. The new tasks are tracing lines and shapes (S3), and tracing letters and numbers (S4).

T. Spelling

There were only three changes to the Spelling section. The first change involved specification of response for copying words (T3) and spelling words in written form (T6) to include typing as an acceptable form of a response. The second change was the addition of a new task to assess the student's ability to spell his own name (T7).

Y. Gross Motor Skills

During the development of the earlier versions of the ABLLS™-R Protocol, there was no attempt made to sequence the skills included in either the gross motor or fine motor sections. In this current version, data from a sample of both typically developing children and children with a developmental delays has been used to place these tasks in a sequence consistent with the observations of the motor skills from the sample of children.

Two new skills have been included in this updated version of the gross motor section. The new skills include the ability to toss and catch a ball (Y24) and to kick a moving ball (Y26).

Z. Fine Motor Skills

There were no new tasks added to the previous list of fine motor skills. As described in the gross motor section, no attempt was made to sequence the fine motor skills in the previous version. The fine motor skills have been placed in a sequence consistent with the skills demonstrated by the sample of children comprised of both typically developing children and children with developmental delays.

COOPERATION AND REINFORCER EFFECTIVENESS

Orig. Task	New Task	TASK NAME	NOTES
A 1	A 1	Take reinforcer when offered	Changed criteria - responds within 3 seconds
A 2	A 2	Take a reinforcer from two choices of items	Changed criteria - responds within 3 seconds
A 3	A 3	Look at a non-reinforcing item	Changed criteria - 6 positions in 10 seconds
A 4	A 4	Take a common object when offered	Changed criteria - responds within 3 seconds
	A 5	**Approaches when reinforcement for required response**	**New - approach when a response is required**
A 5	A 6	Responds to instructor controlled reinforcers	
	A 7	**Responds for multiple instructors**	**New - Generalization issue (Same P 2)**
	A 8	**Waits without touching stimuli**	**New - sit quietly**
	A 9	**Looks to instructor for instruction**	**New - attend to verbal stimuli**
	A 10	**Scans items in array before responding**	**New - scan nonverbal stimuli**
	A 11	**Responds quickly when given an instruction**	**New - short latency**
A 6	A 12	Variation in reinforcement (non-edible)	
A 7	A 13	Intermittent tangible reinforcement	
	A 14	**Instructor interaction reinforcement**	**New - interaction with instructor as reinforcement**
	A 15	**Looks for instructor's change in facial expression and voice**	**New - seeks feedback**
A 8	A 16	Responds to social reinforcers	
A 11	A 17	Waits appropriately if reinforcer delivery is delayed	
A 9	A 18	Seeks approval for task completion	
A 10	A 19	Task completion serves as reinforcer	

VISUAL PERFORMANCE

Orig. Task	New Task	TASK NAME	NOTES
B 10	B 1	Puzzle with a single-piece type of inset	
B 9	B 2	Form box	
B 1	B 3	Match identical **objects** to sample	Changed criterion
B 4	B 4	Match objects to pictures	
B 2	B 5	Match identical pictures to sample	Changed criterion
B 3	B 6	Match pictures to objects	
	B 7	**Fluent matching**	**New - Fluency**
B 5	B 8	Sort non-identical items	Changed criterion
B 6	B 9	Block designs on picture card	Changed wording in criterion
B 11	B 10	Puzzles with multiple connecting pieces in an inset-type frame	
B 12	B 11	Puzzles with a square-edged border frame	
B 7	B 12	Block designs from picture	
B 8	B 13	Sequence pattern to match a visual model	
B 13	B 14	Puzzles with multiple pieces which must be juxtaposed	
B 14	**B 15**	Jigsaw puzzles	
	B 16	**Match associated pictures**	**New**
	B 17	**Sort by function**	**New**
	B 18	**Sort by feature**	**New**
	B 19	**Sort by class**	**New**
B 15	B 20	Delayed replication of a sequence	
B 16	B 21	Delayed finding a sample	Changed criterion
B 17	B 22	Extend a sequence pattern	Changed examples in objective
B 18	B 23	Replicate simple 3-dimensional objects	
	B 24	**Dependent matching sequence**	**New - matching along with the actions of others**
B 19	B 25	Seriation	
B 20	B 26	Picture sequences	
B 21	B 27	Mazes	

RECEPTIVE LANGUAGE

Orig. Task	New Task	TASK NAME	NOTES
C 1	C 1	Responds to own name	Changed criterion
C 2	C 2	Follow instructions to do an enjoyable action in context	Changed criterion
C 3	C 3	Follow instructions to look at a reinforcing item	Changed criterion
C 5	C 4	Follow instructions to touch a reinforcing item in various positions	Changed criterion
C 6	C 5	Follow instructions to touch a common item in various positions	Changed criterion
C 7	C 6	Follow instructions to do an enjoyable action out of context	Changed criterion
C 8	C 7	Follow instructions in routine situations	Changed criteria
C 9	C 8	Follow instructions to give a named, non-reinforcing object	Changed criteria
C 10	C 9	Follow instructions to do a simple motor action	Changed criteria
C 11	C 10	Follow instructions to touch item vs. a distracter	Changed criteria
C 12	C 11	Follow instructions to select one reinforcing item from an array of two objects	Changed criteria
C 13	C 12	Follow instructions to select one of two reinforcing items	Changed criteria
C 14	C 13	Follow instructions to select one of two common objects	
C 15	C 14	Select one of two pictures of common items	
C 17	C 15	Touch own body parts	
C 23	C 16	Select one of six or more objects on a table	Changed criteria
C 24	C 17	Select one of six or more pictures on a table	Changed criteria
C 35	C 18	Acquires new selection skills without intensive training	
	C 19	**Fluent receptive discriminations**	**New - Fluency**
C 16	C 20	Varied instructions to select using any response	
C 18	C 21	Point to body parts on others or pictures	
C 19	C 22	Touch own pieces of clothing	
	C 23	**Touches parts of items**	**New**
C 40	C 24	Select adjectives	
	C 25	**Selects items by following another's gaze**	**New**
	C 26	**Follows hand signals**	**New**
C 27	C 27	Follow an instruction to go to a person	
C 28	C 28	Follow an instruction to give an item to a person or place item on an object	

RECEPTIVE LANGUAGE (Continued)

Orig. Task	New Task	TASK NAME	NOTES
C 29	C 29	Follow an instruction to walk to someone and get a named item	
C 30	C 30	Follow an instruction to go to a person and do an action	
C 31	C 31	Specific motor responses in receptive tasks	
C 32	C 32	Demonstrates a specified action with an object when given different objects	
	C 33	**Multiple actions with an object**	**New**
C 33	C 34	Demonstrates a specified pretend action	
C 34	C 35	Select one of three pictures representing actions	
C 44	C 36	Select associated pictures	
C 20	C 37	Select by function	Changed criteria
C 21	C 38	Select by feature	Changed criteria
C 22	C 39	Select by class	Changed criteria
C 25	C 40	Select two **items** from a larger set	NOTE- changed from only objects to objects or pictures (items)
C 26	C 41	Select two items **in sequence** from a larger set	NOTE- Changed to include pick two **items** in sequence (objects or pictures)
C 36	C 42	Select community helpers	
C 37	C 43	Locate objects in larger, complex picture	
C 38	C 44	Locate objects from parts of objects in larger, complex picture	
C 39	C 45	Select common environmental sounds	
	C 46	**Selects all examples of an item**	**New**
C 41	C 47	Select single items with two specified characteristics	
C 42	C 48	Select set of items with a specified characteristic	
C 43	C 49	Select set of items with two specified characteristics	
C 45	C 50	Follows a multiple component sequence instruction	Changed wording of criteria
C 47	C 51	Receptive prepositions	
C 48	C 52	Receptive pronouns	
C 50	C 53	Select pictures representing a location or an activity presented in a scene	
C 51	C 54	Selects pictures representing emotions	
C 46	C 55	Selects "same" and "different"	
C 49	C 56	Select non-examples	Changed criteria
C 52	C 57	Selects pictures of social interactions	
C 4		Follow instructions to look at a common item	DELETED

IMITATION

Orig. Task	New Task	TASK NAME	NOTES
D 1	D 1	Motor imitation using objects	
D 2	D 2	Motor imitation using objects in a discrimination	Modified examples
D 3	D 3	Motor imitation of gross motor movement with verbal prompts	
D 4	D 4	Imitation of leg and foot movements	
D 5	D 5	Imitation of arm and hand movements	
	D 6	**Imitation discriminating static and kinetic motor movements**	**New**
	D 7	**Varied imitation instructions**	**New - varied instructions**
	D 8	**Imitation of gross motor actions modeled in a mirror**	**New**
D 6	**D 9**	Imitation of head movements	
D 7	D 10	Imitation of mouth and tongue movements	
	D 11	**Imitation of facial/oral motor movements modeled in a mirror**	**New**
D 9	D 12	Motor Imitation of fine motor movement	
	D 13	**Imitation of touching objects in sequence**	**New**
	D 14	**Imitation of blowing**	**New**
	D 15	**Imitate speed of an ongoing action with objects**	**New**
	D 16	**Imitate speed of a recently modeled action with objects**	**New**
D 8	D 17	Imitate speed of an action	
	D 18	**Imitation of touching objects in sequence following a model**	**New**
	D 19	**Imitation of a sequence of actions switching with model**	**New - Fluency Issue**
D 10	D 20	Imitation of a sequence of actions	Changed wording in question
	D 21	**Imitation of intensity of an action**	**New**
	D 22	**Imitation of the number of repetitions of a motor movement**	**New**
	D 23	**Simultaneous imitation of motor movement and a vocalization**	**New**
	D 24	**Motor imitation sequence using multiple objects**	**New**
D 11	D 25	Imitates motor movement without a direct verbal prompt	
D 12	D 26	Spontaneously imitates the actions of others	
D 13	D 27	Delayed imitation	

VOCAL IMITATION

Orig. Task	New Task	TASK NAME	NOTES
E 1	E 1	Imitates sounds on request	
	E 2	**Imitates sequence of single sounds switching with a model**	**New - Fluency issue**
E 2	E 3	Imitates initial sounds of words	
	E 4	**Imitation of multiple separate sound combinations**	**New - Discrimination issue**
	E 5	**Imitation of short & fast vs. elongated/slow sounds**	**New**
	E 6	**Imitation of the number of repetitions of a sound**	**New**
	E 7	**Imitation of a held sound to a second sound**	**New**
	E 8	**Consonant-vowel/ vowel-consonant combinations**	**New**
	E 9	**Consonant-vowel-consonant-vowel**	**New**
	E 10	**Consonant-vowel-consonant combinations**	**New**
E 3	E 11	Imitates consonant blends	Modified examples
E 4	E 12	Imitation of words on request	
E 5	E 13	Imitation of phrases on request	
E 6	E 14	Imitation of number sequences on request	
	E 15	**Imitation of short & fast vs. elongated/slow words**	**New**
	E 16	**Imitation of loud vs. soft sounds and words**	**New**
	E 17	**Imitation of low vs. high sounds and words**	**New**
	E 18	**Repeat short message to another person**	**New**
E 8	E 19	Spontaneous imitation of words	
E 9	E 20	Spontaneous imitation of phrases	
E 7		Prosody	Separated into individual items

The ABLLS™-R Update Summary

REQUESTS

Orig. Task	New Task	TASK NAME	NOTES
F 1	F 1	Requests by indicating	Scoring criteria clarified
F 2	F 2	Multiply controlled requests	Scoring criteria clarified
F 3	F 3	Requesting with the reinforcer present and when asked "What do you want?"	Scoring criteria clarified
F 4	F 4	Requesting when asked "What do you want?"	Scoring criteria clarified
F 5	F 5	Spontaneous requests with items present (No prompts)	Modified
	F 6	**Spontaneouss requests items not present**	**New**
	F 7	**Requests with eye contact**	**New**
F 6	F 8	Request others to perform an action	
F 8	F 9	Requests missing items needed for a task	
F 9	F 10	Requests with head movements or by saying Yes/No	
F 10	F 11	Requests using sentences	Changed criteria
F 11	F 12	Requests help	New examples
F 26	F 13	Acquires novel requests without intensive training	
F 7	F 14	Requests attention	
F 12	F 15	Request others to remove an item or stop an activity	
F 22	F 16	Requests using adjectives	
F 23	F 17	Requests using prepositions	
F 21	F 18	Requests future items or events	
F 13	F 19	Requests information using "**What**"	New examples
F 14	F 20	Requests information using "**Where**"	New examples
F 15	F 21	Requests information using "**Who/Whose**"	
F 24	F 22	Requests using adverbs	
F 25	F 23	Requests using pronouns	
F 16	F 24	Requests information using "**Which**"	
F 17	F 25	Requests information using "**When**"	
F 18	F 26	Requests information using "**How**"	
F 19	F 27	Requests information using "**Can,**" "**Do,**" "**Does,**" or "**Will**"	
F 20	F 28	Requests information using "**Why**"	
F 27	F 29	Spontaneous requests	

LABELING

Orig. Task	New Task	TASK NAME	NOTES
G 1	G 1	Labels reinforcers	
G 2	G 2	Labels common objects	
G 3	G 3	Labels common people (actual individuals, not professionals)	
G 4	G 4	Labels **pictures** of common items	
G9	G5	Labels body parts	
C 19	**G 6**	**Labels pieces of clothing**	**New**
G 5	G 7	Labels common ongoing actions	
G 6	G 8	Labels pictures of common actions	
	G 9	**Fluent labeling**	**New - Fluency**
G7	G 10	Acquires novel labels without intensive training	Changed objective
G 8	G 11	Labels items using a carrier phrase	
G10	G 12	Labels parts or features of objects	Changed critera
G11	G 13	Labels adjectives	
	G 14	**Label associated pictures**	**New**
G 12	G 15	Labels item when told its **function**	Changed critera
G 13	G 16	Labels item when told one of its **features**	
G 14	G 17	Labels item when told its **class**	
G 22	G 18	Two-component labels (nouns) with objects	
G 23	G 19	Two-component labels (nouns) with pictures	
G 24	G 20	Labels two-component with carrier phrase	
G 25	G 21	Two-component labels (noun verb)	
G 26	G 22	Two-component labels (noun adjective)	
G 18	G 23	Labels by indicating Yes/No	
G 15	G 24	Labels function of an item	Changed criteria
G 16	G 25	Labels class of an object	
	G 26	**Discrimination of question to label aspects of items**	**New**
G 17	G 27	Labels the class of a set of items	
G 19	G 28	Labels features of items which are missing or incorrect	
G 20	G 29	Labels exclusion from a category (negation)	Changed criteria
G 21	G 30	Identifies obvious problems	
G 27	G 31	Labels community helpers	
	G 32	**Labels items at a distance when others point to it**	**New**
G 28	G 33	Labels common environmental sounds	
G 29	G 34	Uses carrier phrase when labeling nouns with verbs or adjectives.	

LABELING (Continued)

Orig. Task	New Task	TASK NAME	NOTES
G 30	G 35	Labels prepositions	
G 31	G 36	Uses carrier phrases when using prepositions	
G 32	G 37	Labels pronouns	
G 33	G 38	Uses carrier phrases when using pronouns	
G 36	G 39	Labels and describes events or items presented in a scene	
G 37	G 40	Naming specified parts of scenes	
G 38	G 41	Labels adverbs	
G 39	G 42	Labels emotions of others	
G 40	G 43	Internal events and emotions	
G 34	G 44	Multiple component naming (three component labels)	
G 35	G 45	Labels (three component +) with carrier phrase	
G 41	G 46	Labels social interaction behavior	
G 42	G 47	Spontaneous labeling	

INTRAVERBAL

Orig. Task	New Task	TASK NAME	NOTES
H 1	H 1	Fill in words from songs	
H 2	H 2	Fill in blanks regarding fun items and activities	
H 3	H 3	Sign English words (students who use ASL)	
H 4	H 4	Animal sounds	
H 5	H 5	Answers questions regarding personal information	
H 6	H 6	Fill in words describing common activities	
	H 7	**Intraverbal associations**	**New**
H 7	H 8	Fill in item given function	
H 8	H 9	Fill in function given item	
	H 10	Answers **"What"** questions regarding items found in home	**New**
	H 11	Answers **"What"** questions regarding functions	**New**
	H 12	Answers "**Where**" questions regarding items found in home or classroom	**New Note: now split to 2 items**
	H 13	Answers "**Where**" questions regarding activities done at home or school	**New Note: now split to 2 items**
H 12	H 14	Fill in item given the class	
H 13	H 15	Multiple responses given specific categories	
H 9	H 16	Fill in features given the item	
H 10	H 17	Fill in item given its feature	
H 11	H 18	Fill in class given the item	
	H 19	**Name items previously observed**	**New Note: now split to 3 items**
	H 20	**Name previously observed activities**	**New Note: now split to 3 items**
	H 21	**Name people previously observed**	**New Note: now split to 3 items**
H 24	H 22	With visual display, makes related statements (not naming)	
	H 23	**Answers "What" questions relevant to items found in the community**	**New**
	H 24	**Answers "What" questions relevant to activites that he can do in the community**	**New**
	H 25	**Answers "Where" questions regarding activities and items found in the community**	**New**
H 34	H 26	Answers questions with **multiple responses** concerning his immediate community	
H 14	H 27	States class given multiple class members (examples)	
H 19	H 28	Answers "**Who/Whose**" questions	
H 21	H 29	Answers "**When**" questions	
	H 30	**Discrimination of questions asked about items and activities**	**New**

INTRAVERBAL (Continued)

Orig. Task	New Task	TASK NAME	NOTES
H 20	H 31	Answers "**Which**" questions	
H 22	H 32	Answers "**How**" questions	
H 23	H 33	Answers "**Why**" questions	
H 25	H 34	Describes steps in sequence of a daily activity	
H 26	H 35	States activity when told sequence of actions	
H 27	H 36	States item when told its functions, features, or class (multiple features)	New Description
H 28	H 37	Intraverbal Yes/No with "Can," "Do," "Does," or "Will" questions	
H 29	H 38	Answers questions containing two critical stimuli (multiple component questions with **multiple responses**)	
H 30	H 39	Answers questions containing three critical stimuli (multiple component questions with **multiple responses**)	
	H 40	**Describes items**	**New**
H 31	H 41	Describes steps before and after in sequence of a daily activity	
H 32	H 42	Answers questions concerning past and upcoming events	
H 39	H 43	Maintains a conversation with an adult or peer	Changed criteria
H 40	H 44	Answers **novel** questions	
H 35	H 45	Answers questions relevant to current events	
H 36	H 46	Answers questions with multiple responses concerning current events	
	H 47	**Answers questions with multiple responses in group discussions**	**New**
H 42	H 48	Tells about experiences/ Tells stories	Changed example for clarification
H 41	H 49	Spontaneous conversation	
H 15		Provides opposites when given comparison stimulus	Deleted
H 16		Answers "**What**" questions	Note: now split to 4 items
H 17		Answers "**Where**" questions	Note: now split to 3 items
H 18		Name items previously observed	New Note: now split to 3 items
H 33		Answers questions relevant to events in their immediate community Single Responses	New Note: now split to 3 items
H 37		Answers questions re: academic material	Deleted
H 38		Multiple responses to questions relevant to academic material	Deleted

SPONTANEOUS VOCALIZATIONS

Orig. Task	New Task	TASK NAME	NOTES
I 1	I 1	Vocalize identifiable speech sounds	Modified - now specifies speech sounds
I 2	I 2	Spontaneously says words or approximations to	
I 3	I 3	Spontaneously says phrases	
I 4	I 4	Sings songs with models	
I 5	I 5	Sing songs	
I 6	I 6	Spontaneous vocal imitation	
I 7	I 7	Spontaneous requests	
I 8	I 8	Spontaneous labeling	
I 9	I 9	Spontaneous conversation	

SYNTAX & GRAMMAR

Orig. Task	New Task	TASK NAME	NOTES
J 1	J 1	Mean length of response	No changes in this section
J 2	J 2	Syntax (Word order)	
J 3	J 3	Articles	
J 4	J 4	Verbs-present progressive	
J 5	J 5	Regular plurals	
J 6	J 6	Verbs-irregular past tense	
J 7	J 7	Contractions	
J 8	J 8	Is/am with "ing" verb	
J 9	J 9	Verbs-regular past tense	
J 10	J 10	Possessive "S"	
J 11	J 11	Negatives	
J 12	J 12	Locatives	
J 13	J 13	Future tense	
J 14	J 14	Conjunctions	
J 15	J 15	Irregular Plurals	
J 16	J 16	Comparatives	
J 17	J 17	Demonstratives	
J 18	J 18	Label strength of a verbal response	
J 19	J 19	Quantification of a verbal response	
J 20	J 20	Label emotional state associated with a verbal response	

Please do not duplicate

PLAY & LEISURE SKILLS

Orig. Task	New Task	TASK NAME	NOTES
K 1	K 1	Explores toys in the environment	
	K 2	**Allows others to manipulate/ touch toys**	New
K 10	K 3	Independent outdoor activities	Changed criteria and removed games Play "Tag"; "Duck, Duck Goose"; "catch"
K 8	K 4	Independent **indoor** leisure activities	
K 2	K 5	Plays with toys/ manipulates toys as designed	
K 4	K 6	Independently plays with toys and engages in verbal behavior	
K 3	K 7	Multiple responses with toys related to a theme	
K 5	K 8	Plays interactively with others students	Changed criteria - removed allow others to be near - allows other students to be near them when playing with a toy
	K 9	**Plays interactively with a variety of peers**	New
K 7	K 10	Sociodramatic play	Clarified criteria to include "activites"
K 6	K 11	Plays with toys and talks with peers	
	K 12	**Plays simple ball games**	New
	K 13	**Coordinated play with peers**	New
	K 14	**Interactive motor games**	New
K 9	K 15	Board games	Changed task name from -Appropriate interactive leisure activities & removed dress-up in old clothes
K 10		Outdoor games and activities	SPLIT independent outdoor & interactive
K 5		Plays interactively with others students	Change criteria from allow others vs specific interaction
K 9		Appropriate interactive leisure activities	Change to Board games & move the dress-up

SOCIAL INTERACTION SKILLS

Orig. Task	New Task	TASK NAME	NOTES
L 1	L 1	Appropriate when near peers or siblings	
L 7	L 2	Takes offered items	Changed criteria
L 2	L 3	Tolerates/ responds appropriately to positive touches by peers or siblings	Note clarified what is the behavior of concern & more specific example
L 3	L 4	Shows interest in the behavior of others	Added examples
L 12	L 5	Looks at others to start a social interaction	
L 13	L 6	Physically approaches and engages others	Changed criteria and description - no obvious reinforcer - deleted prompts
	L 7	**Looks at others in anticipation of completing a reinforcing action**	**New - joint attention**
L 5	L 8	Listener-receptive	Changed description and criteria
L 6	L 9	Imitates peers	
L 10	L 10	Returns greetings	
L 14	L 11	Physically prompts others to do activities	
L 4	L 12	Responds to approaches & attempts to interact from peers	
L 17	L 13	Sharing-gives-up items to others	
	L 14	**Searches for missing person**	**New**
	L 15	**Active attention seeking**	**New**
L 21	L 16	Labels items for others	
L 9	L 17	Eye contact	
L 15	L 18	Asks peers for items (single)	
L 16	L 19	Sharing -asks for items to be shared	
L 18	L 20	Sharing-offers items to others	
L 11	L 21	Initiates greetings	
	L 22	**Joins peers in an activity**	**New**
	L 23	**Observation of peers' attention to activities**	**New**
	L 24	**Feedback from peers**	**New- "too close" "too loud"**
	L 25	**Adjusts behavior based on changes in peer's actions**	**New**
	L 26	**Assists other to participate**	**New**
	L 27	**States what others like/dislike**	**New**
	L 28	**Direct others attention to something of interest them**	**New**
	L 29	**Attends to interests of others**	**New**
	L 30	**Delivers a message**	**New**
	L 31	**Waits for break into conversation**	**New**
L 19	L 32	Converses with others	
L 20	L 33	Asks for information	
L 22	L 34	Obtains and maintains attention of others	Changed criteria & task name
L 8	L 8	Sharing-accepts offers/invitation to join	**DELETED**

GROUP INSTRUCTION

Orig. Task	New Task	TASK NAME	NOTES
M 1	M 1	Sits appropriately in small group	New examples given re: disruptive B
M 2	M 2	Sits appropriately in large group	New examples given re: disruptive B
M 3	M 3	Attends to teacher in group	
M 4	M 4	Attends to other students in group	
M 6	M 5	Follows group instructions- all do the same receptive response	Changed criteria
M 7	M 6	Follows group instructions with a discrimination	Changed criteria
M 5	M 7	Raises hand to get teacher attention to do an activity	Changed objective
M 8	M 8	Raises hand **to** answer a question	
M 9	M 9	Raises hand AND names item	Changed criteria
M 10	M 10	Raises hand AND answers a question	Changed criteria
M 11	M 11	Takes turns during instruction	
M 12	M 12	Learns new skills in group teaching format	

FOLLOW CLASSROOM ROUTINES

Orig. Task	New Task	TASK NAME	NOTES
N 10	N 1	Follows daily routines (backpack, etc.)	
N 4	N 2	Works independently on non-academic activities	
N 7	N 3	Sits and waits appropriately during transitions	
N 6	N 4	Physically transitions to next area or activity	
N 9	N 5	Waits turn to do activities (wash hands, etc.)	
N 1	N 6	Gets in line on request	
N 5	N 7	Works independently on academic activities	
N 2	N 8	Gets & returns own materials	
N 3	N 9	Completes a task and brings work to teacher or puts away materials	
N 8	N 10	Stands and waits appropriately during transitions	

GENERALIZED RESPONDING

Orig. Task	New Task	TASK NAME	NOTES
P 1	P 1	Generalizes across stimuli	No changes in this section
P 2	P 2	Generalizes across instructors	
P 3	P 3	Generalizes across environments	
P 4	P 4	Use of skills in groups	
P 5	P 5	Generalized response forms	
P 6	P 6	Generalization of language skills	

READING SKILLS

Orig. Task	New Task	TASK NAME	NOTES
Q 1	Q 1	Receptive letters	
Q 2	Q 2	Labels letters	
Q 3	Q 3	Receptive sounds of letters	
Q 4	Q 4	Labels sounds of letters	
Q 5	Q 5	Match words with pictures	
Q 6	Q 6	Match words to words	change in criterion
Q 7	Q 7	Names letters in words reading left to right	
Q 8	Q 8	Match individual letters to letters on word card	
Q 9	Q9	Fill in missing letter of words	
Q 10	Q 10	Read simple words	
Q 11	Q 11	Decode words	change in criterion
Q 12	Q 12	Read small groups of words from left to right	
Q 13	Q 13	Read simple sentences (3-6 words)	
Q 14	Q 14	Fills-in missing words	
	Q 15	**Reads and follows simple instructions to do actions**	New
	Q 16	**Reads and follows simple instructions on worksheets**	New
Q 15	Q 17	Read passages and answer comprehension questions	

The ABLLS™-R Update Summary

MATH SKILLS

Orig. Task	New Task	TASK NAME	NOTES
R 1	R 1	Rote counts with prompts	
R 2	R 2	Rote counting	
R 3	R 3	Count objects with prompts	change in criterion
R 4	R 4	Count given objects	change in criterion
R 5	R 5	Count out objects from a larger set	
R 6	R 6	Names numerals in sequence	
R 7	R 7	Names numbers	
R 8	R 8	Match number with same amount of objects	
R 23	**R 9**	**"more" receptive & labels**	combined receptive & label
R 25	**R 10**	**"less" receptive & labels**	combined receptive & label
R 29	**R 11**	**"some" receptive & labels**	combined receptive & label
R 31	**R 12**	**"all" receptive & labels**	combined receptive & label
R 41	**R 13**	**"zero/none" receptive & labels**	combined receptive & label
R 9	R 14	Add items to specified quantity	
R 15	**R 15**	**"same" receptive & labels**	combined receptive & label
R 17	**R 16**	**"different" receptive & labels**	combined receptive & label
R 27	**R 17**	**"greater" receptive & labels**	combined receptive & label
R 33	**R 18**	**"add" receptive & labels**	combined receptive & label
	R 19	**Gets specified number of identical items**	**New**
R 10	R 20	Add numbers	
R 11	R 21	Time telling	
R 12	R 22	Identify coins by name	
R 13	R 23	Identify all coins by value	
R 14	R 24	Interchange coins to arrive at equal values	changed criterion
R 19	R 25	"equal" receptive & labels	combined receptive & label
R 21	R 26	"unequal" receptive & labels	combined receptive & label
R 35	R 27	"minus" receptive & labels	combined receptive & label
R 37	R 28	"plus" receptive & labels	combined receptive & label
R 39	R 29	"subtract/take away" receptive & labels	combined receptive & label

MATH SKILLS (Continued)

Orig. Task	New Task	TASK NAME	NOTES
		DELETED	
R 16		Labels "same"	Combined with receptive
R 18		Labels "different"	Combined with receptive
R 20		Labels "equal"	Combined with receptive
R 22		Labels "unequal"	Combined with receptive
R 24		Labels "more"	Combined with receptive
R 26		Labels "less"	Combined with receptive
R 28		Labels "greater"	Combined with receptive
R 30		Labels "some"	Combined with receptive
R 32		Labels "all"	Combined with receptive
R 34		Labels "add"	Combined with receptive
R 36		Labels "minus"	Combined with receptive
R 38		Labels "plus"	Combined with receptive
R 40		Labels "subtract/take away"	Combined with receptive
R 42		Labels "zero/none"	Combined with receptive

WRITING SKILLS

Orig. Task	New Task	TASK NAME	NOTES
S 1	S 1	Mark on paper	
S 2	S 2	Color between lines	
S 3	S 3	Trace lines and shapes	**Split into 2 items from old S3**
S 3	S 4	Trace letters and numbers	**Split into 2 items from old S3**
S 4	S 5	Copy straight lines	
S 5	S 6	Copy curved lines	
S 6	S 7	Copy letters (with sample)	
S 7	S 8	Copy numbers (with sample)	
S 8	S 9	Print letters	
S 9	S 10	Print numbers	

SPELLING

Orig. Task	New Task	TASK NAME	NOTES
T 1	T 1	Match individual letters to letters on word card	
T 2	T 2	Fill in missing letter of words	
T 3	T 3	Copy words	Changed to include typing as a response form
T 4	T 4	Writes in missing letter of words	
T 5	T 5	Spell words vocally	
T 6	T 6	Spell words in a written form	Changed to include typing as a response form
	T 7	**Spell own name**	**New**

DRESSING SKILLS

Orig. Task	New Task	TASK NAME	NOTES
U 1	U 1	Pants up & down	
U 2	U 2	Shoes on and off	
U 3	U 3	Pullover shirts on and take off	
U 4	U 4	Buttoning shirts on and off	
U 5	U 5	Pants on and off	
U 6	U 6	Socks on and off	
U 7	U 7	Coat on and off	
U 9	U 8	Unzip zipper	
U 10	U 9	Fasten zipper	
U 11	U 10	Use zipper on clothes	
U 12	U 11	Fasten buttons	
U 13	U 12	Use snaps	
U 14	U 13	Use buckles	
U 15	U 14	Adjust clothing when needed	
U 8	U 15	Tie shoes	

EATING SKILLS

Orig. Task	New Task	TASK NAME	NOTES
V 1	V 1	Eat finger foods	
V 2	V 2	Drink from a straw	
V 3	V 3	Drink from a cup	
V 4	V 4	Feed self with a spoon and fork	
V 5	V 5	Spread with a knife	
V 6	V 6	Pour liquid into a cup	
V 7	V 7	Cut food with a knife	
V 8	V 8	Take prepared lunch to table	
V 9	V 9	Clean-up table after meals	
V 10	V 10	Keep eating areas clean	

GROOMING SKILLS

Orig. Task	New Task	TASK NAME	NOTES
W 1	W 1	Wash hands	No changes in this section
W 2	W 2	Dry hands	
W 3	W 3	Wash face	
W 4	W 4	Dry face	
W 5	W 5	Comb or brush hair	
W 6	W 6	Brush teeth	
W 7	W 7	Blow nose when needed	

TOILETING SKILLS

Orig. Task	New Task	TASK NAME	NOTES
X 1	X 1	Urinate in toilet	
X 2	X 2	Remain dry (urine) on a toileting schedule	Changed criteria
X 3	X 3	Independently use familiar restroom for urination	
X 4	X 4	Requests to use toilet when needed	
X 5	X 5	Wipe self after urinating (Females)	Changed Criteria
X 6	X 6	Defecate in toilet	
X 7	X 7	Remain clean (bowel movement) on a toileting schedule	
X 8	X 8	Wipe self after bowel movement	
X 9	X 9	Independently use familiar restroom for bowel movements	
X 10	X 10	Use restroom without assistance	

GROSS MOTOR SKILLS

Orig. Task	New Task	TASK NAME	NOTES
Y 3	Y 1	Walk forward with appropriate gait	
Y 2	Y 2	Kneel	
Y 6	Y 3	Run smoothly	
Y 8	Y 4	Roll sideways	
Y 12	Y 5	Jump forward	
Y 13	Y 6	Jump down	
Y 4	Y 7	Walk backward	
Y 9	Y 8	Hop on two feet	
Y 16	Y 9	Throw ball from chest or overhand	
Y 21	Y 10	Roll a ball	
Y 25	Y 11	Climb a ladder using reciprocal motion	
Y 1	Y 12	Creep on stomach	
Y 7	Y 13	Squat	
Y 26	Y 14	Walk across a balance beam	
Y 18	Y 15	Catch a ball any method	
Y 22	Y 16	Ride a tricycle	
Y 5	Y 17	Walk sideways	
Y 11	Y 18	Gallop	
Y 14	Y 19	Balance on one foot	
Y 15	Y 20	Kick ball at target	
Y 28	Y 21	Hang from bar	
Y 19	Y 22	Catch a ball in hands	
Y 17	Y 23	Throw ball underhand	
	Y 24	**Toss and catch a ball**	**New**
Y 20	Y 25	Bounce a ball	
	Y 26	**Kick a moving ball**	**New**
Y 27	Y 27	Pump while swinging	
Y 10	Y 28	Skip	
Y 24	Y 29	Jumping jacks	
Y 23	Y 30	Ride a bicycle	

FINE MOTOR SKILLS

Orig. Task	New Task	TASK NAME	NOTES
Z 17	Z 1	Mark on paper with a crayon	Changes to sequence of skills
Z 1	Z 2	Places objects in a form box	
Z 3	Z 3	Single-piece inset puzzle	
Z 4	Z 4	Multiple puzzle pieces into a frame	
Z 6	Z 5	Blocks on block design cards	
Z 8	Z 6	Transfer objects to the opposite hand	
Z 2	Z 7	Places pegs in a peg board	
Z 26	Z 8	Turns pages of a book	
Z 9	Z 9	Clothespins on a line	
Z 18	Z 10	Color within boundaries	
Z 14	Z 11	Open "Ziplock" type bags	
Z 15	Z 12	Snips with scissors	
Z 5	Z 13	Stacks blocks	
Z 10	Z 14	Strings beads	
Z 11	Z 15	Remove lids of jars	
Z 21	Z 16	Cuts across paper with scissors	
Z 25	Z 17	Trace lines with a finger	
Z 28	Z 18	Squeezes glue from a bottle	
Z 13	Z 19	Remove wrappers	
Z 19	Z 20	Roughly copy shapes and patterns	
Z 23	Z 21	Paste shapes on outlined picture	
Z 24	Z 22	Paste shapes on plain paper picture	
Z 7	Z 23	Objects (rings) on pegs	
Z 12	Z 24	Replace lids of jars	
Z 16	Z 25	Uses pincer grip	
Z 27	Z 26	Fold a piece of paper	
Z 22	Z 27	Cuts out shapes	
Z 20	Z 28	Accurately copy shapes and patterns	

Appendix 2: Skills Tracking Grids and Sample IEP for an "Early Learner"

Assessment of Basic Language and Learning Skills - Revised
Skill Tracking System

Student: _____

Assessor	Date	Color Code
JP	5/06	

Early Learner Profile

Copyright © 1994-2006 By Behavior Analysts, Inc.   Please do not duplicate

Cooperation & Reinforcer Effectiveness
A1–A19

Visual Performance
B1–B27

Receptive Language
C1–C57

Imitation
D1–D27

Vocal Imitation
E1–E20

Requests
F1–F29

Labeling
G1–G47

Intraverbals
H1–H49

Spontaneous Vocalizations
I1–I9

Assessment of Basic Language and Learning Skills - Revised
Skill Tracking System

Student:

Early Learner Profile

Assessor	Date	Color Code
JP	5/06	

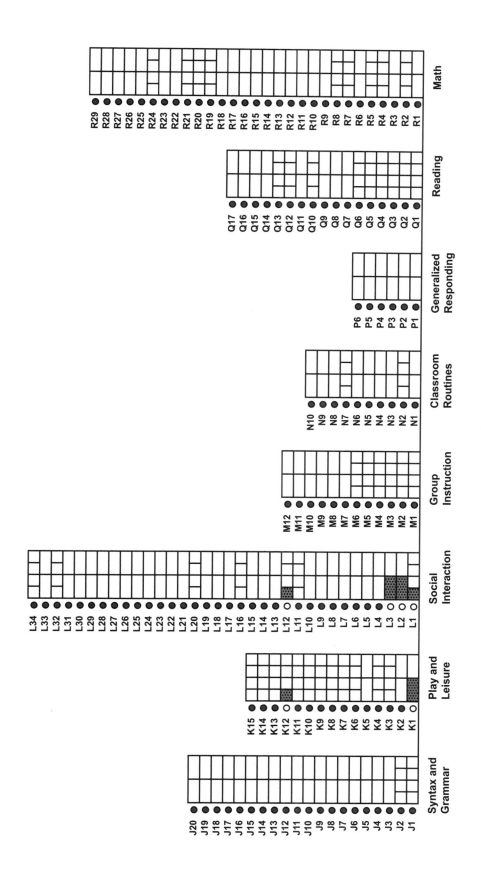

Assessment of Basic Language and Learning Skills - Revised
Skill Tracking System

Student:

Assessor: JP

Early Learner Profile

Date: 5/06

Color Code

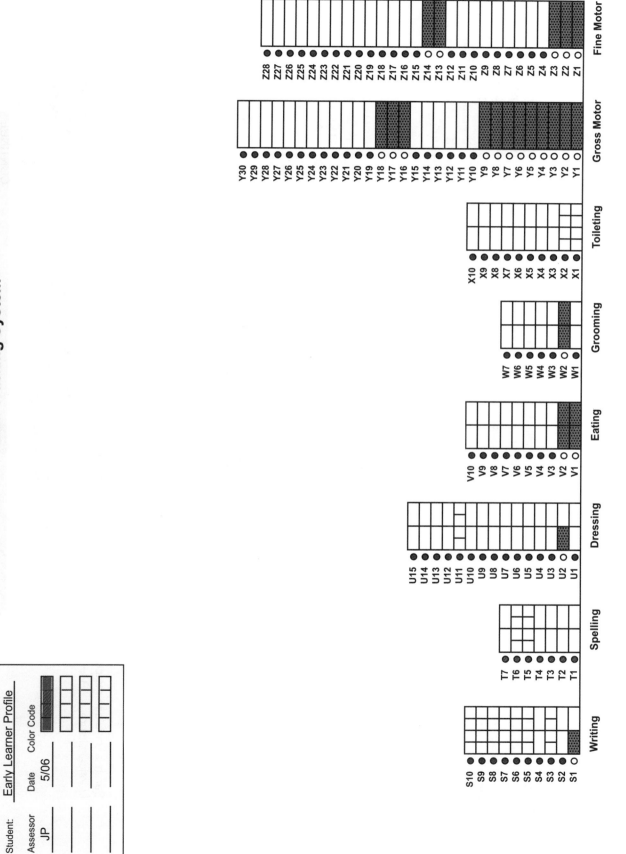

Appendix 2: Sample "Early Learner" IEP

CURRENT LEVEL

OBJECTIVE

Visual Performance

CRITERIA

Sarah is able to match 2 blocks to one block design card (by placing them on top of the design card) and is able to put 4 pieces into a form box by "looking and locating" the appropriate hole for the piece. (B9=1 & B2=3)

1 Sarah will be able to match blocks to a design card for up to 5 blocks with no extras. (B9)

As measured by:
_____ Teacher observation
_____ Work Samples
__x__ Data Collection
__80__ % Accuracy Criterion
NEW _x_ MET _____
CONTINUE____ DELETE____

Sarah is able to complete many single inset puzzles and 1 four piece puzzle. (B1=2 & B10=0)

2 Sarah will be able to complete at least 5 interlocking puzzles in a frame with 5 pieces or more. (B10)

As measured by:
_____ Teacher observation
_____ Work Samples
__x__ Data Collection
__80__ % Accuracy Criterion
NEW _x_ MET _____
CONTINUE____ DELETE____

Sarah is unable to match objects to identical objects. (B3=0)

3 When presented with an array of three or more objects and given an object that matches one of those in the display, Sarah will match the object to the appropriate object. (B3)

As measured by:
_____ Teacher observation
_____ Work Samples
__x__ Data Collection
__80__ % Accuracy Criterion
NEW _x_ MET _____
CONTINUE____ DELETE____

Sarah is unable to match objects to identical pictures. (B4=0)

4 When presented with an array of three or more pictures and given an object that is in one of the pictures, Sarah will match the object to the appropriate picture for any picture/object combination. (B4)

As measured by:
_____ Teacher observation
_____ Work Samples
__x__ Data Collection
__80__ % Accuracy Criterion
NEW _x_ MET _____
CONTINUE____ DELETE____

Appendix 2: Sample "Early Learner" IEP

CURRENT LEVEL	#	OBJECTIVE	CRITERIA
		Receptive Language	
Sarah is unable to follow simple instructions (e.g., arms up, clap, etc.). (C9=0)	5	Sarah will follow instructions to do at least 6 simple motor tasks (e.g., clap, turn around, arms up). (C9)	As measured by: ____ Teacher observation ____ Work Samples _x_ Data Collection _80_% Accuracy Criterion NEW _X_ MET ____ CONTINUE____ DELETE____
Sarah is unable to receptively identify objects. (C13=0)	6	Sarah will be able to receptively identify at least 10 items. (C12 & 13)	As measured by: ____ Teacher observation ____ Work Samples _X_ Data Collection ____ Speech Therapist _80_% Accuracy Criterion NEW _X_ MET ____ CONTINUE____ DELETE____
		Imitation	
Sarah is able to imitate 8 actions with objects. (D1=2)	7	Sarah will be able to imitate 15 actions with objects when they are modeled and when instructed to "Do this." (D1)	As measured by: ____ Teacher observation ____ Work Samples _X_ Data Collection _80_% Accuracy Criterion NEW _X_ MET ____ CONTINUE____ DELETE____
Sarah is able to imitate 8 gross motor actions. (D3=2)	8	Sarah will be able to imitate at least 20 gross motor actions (e.g., clap hands, touch tummy, etc.) when they are modeled and when instructed to "Do this." (D3)	As measured by: ____ Teacher observation ____ Work Samples _X_ Data Collection _80_% Accuracy Criterion NEW _X_ MET ____ CONTINUE____ DELETE____

Appendix 2: Sample "Early Learner" IEP

CURRENT LEVEL

Sarah is not able to imitate head, mouth, nor tongue movements. (D9 & D10=0)

Sarah is able to imitate "eee" and "aaa". (E1=1)

Sarah has recently learned the sign for candy and beans. (F3 & 4=1, & F5 & 29=0)

Sarah has recently learned the sign for candy and books but sometimes confuses the two. (F3 & 4=1, & F5 & 29=0)

OBJECTIVE

9   Sarah will be able to imitate at least 5 head, mouth, and/or tongue movements upon request. (D9 & 10)

Vocal Imitation

10   Sarah will imitate at least 5 different sounds upon request. (E1)

Requesting

11   Sarah will request desired items by signs or vocals at least 10 times per day. (F29)

12   Sarah will be able to request at least 10 different items through the use of sign or vocals. (F3, 4, & 5)

CRITERIA

As measured by: ____Teacher ____Work observation _X_Data Collection Samples
_80_% Accuracy Criterion
NEW_X_ MET____
CONTINUE____ DELETE____

As measured by: ____Teacher ____Work observation _X_Data Collection Samples
_80_% Accuracy Criterion
NEW_X_ MET____
CONTINUE____ DELETE____

As measured by: ____Teacher ____Work observation _X_Data Collection Samples
_80_% Accuracy Criterion
NEW_X_ MET____
CONTINUE____ DELETE____

As measured by: ____Teacher ____Work observation _X_Data Collection Samples
Speech Therapist _80_%
Accuracy Criterion NEW_X_
MET____
CONTINUE____ DELETE____

Appendix 2: Sample "Early Learner" IEP

CURRENT LEVEL

Sarah is unable to label any items. G1 & 2=0)

Sarah currently has a low rate of making spontaneous vocalizations. (I1=1)

Sarah will play with toys for short periods of time but she requires multiple physical prompts to play with toys as designed. (K1=2 & K5=0)

Sarah is able to catch and throw a ball, and will sometimes take items that are offered to her by her peers. (K12=1, L1, 2, 3 & 12=1, all other L=0)

OBJECTIVE

Labeling

13   Sarah will be able to label at least 10 items using signs or vocals. (G1 & 2) Note: This objective to be started once Sarah can request and receptively identify at least 10 objects.

Spontaneous Vocalizations

14   Sarah will increase her spontaneous vocalizations that include speech sounds by 50% over baseline levels. (I1)

Play & Social Skills

15   Sarah will be able to play with at least 5 different toys as designed for at least 2 minutes with no more than 2 physical prompts. (K5, & 7)

16   Sarah will roll a ball to another peer or adult for at least three exchanges. (K12, & L4, 9, & 12)

CRITERIA

As measured by: ____Teacher
observation   ____Work
Samples   _X__Data Collection
          ____Speech Therapist   _80_%
Accuracy Criterion   NEW_X__
MET____
CONTINUE____ DELETE____

As measured by: ____Teacher
observation   ____Work
Samples   _X__Data Collection
_80_% Accuracy Criterion
NEW_X__   MET____
CONTINUE____ DELETE____

As measured by: ____Teacher
observation   ____Work
Samples   _X__Data Collection
_80_% Accuracy Criterion
NEW_X__   MET____
CONTINUE____ DELETE____

As measured by: _X__Teacher
observation   ____Work
Samples   ____Data Collection
_80_% Accuracy Criterion
NEW_X__   MET____
CONTINUE____ DELETE____

Appendix 2: Sample "Early Learner" IEP

CURRENT LEVEL	# OBJECTIVE	CRITERIA
	Classroom Routines	
Sarah does not follow any classroom routines without being prompted. (All N=0)	17 Sarah will complete her morning routine e.g., hang up her coat, put lunch box in cubbie, put away backpack, with no more than two verbal prompts. (N1)	As measured by: _X_ Teacher ___ Work observation ___ Data Collection Samples _80_% Accuracy Criterion NEW _X_ MET ___ CONTINUE___ DELETE___
	Self-Help Skills	
Sarah can take off her shoes, but otherwise does not help with any dressing tasks. (U2=1, & all other U=0)	18 Sarah will be able to pull down her pants without assistance for toileting. (U1)	As measured by: _X_ Teacher ___ Work observation ___ Data Collection Samples _80_% Accuracy Criterion NEW _X_ MET ___ CONTINUE___ DELETE___
Sarah can dry her hands when given only a verbal prompt. (W2=1, & all other W=0)	19 Sarah will be able to wash & dry her hands without assistance. (W1 & 2)	As measured by: ___ Teacher ___ Work observation _X_ Data Collection Samples _80_% Accuracy Criterion NEW _X_ MET ___ CONTINUE___ DELETE___
	Fine Motor Skills	
Sarah can mark on paper with a crayon, but can't color within boundaries, nor trace simple lines. (S1=1, S3=0, Z1=1, Z10, 17 & 20=0)	20 Sarah will be able to trace straight lines. (S3)	As measured by: ___ Teacher _X_ Work observation ___ Data Collection Samples _80_% Accuracy Criterion NEW _X_ MET ___ CONTINUE___ DELETE___

Appendix 3: Skills Tracking Grids and Sample IEP for an "Advanced Learner"

Assessment of Basic Language and Learning Skills - Revised
Skill Tracking System

Student: _____

Assessor: JP

Date: 5/06

Advanced Learner Profile

Color Code

Spontaneous Vocalizations — I9 I8 I7 I6 I5 I4 I3 I2 I1

Intraverbals — H49 H48 H47 H46 H45 H44 H43 H42 H41 H40 H39 H38 H37 H36 H35 H34 H33 H32 H31 H30 H29 H28 H27 H26 H25 H24 H23 H22 H21 H20 H19 H18 H17 H16 H15 H14 H13 H12 H11 H10 H9 H8 H7 H6 H5 H4 H3 H2 H1

Labeling — G47 G46 G45 G44 G43 G42 G41 G40 G39 G38 G37 G36 G35 G34 G33 G32 G31 G30 G29 G28 G27 G26 G25 G24 G23 G22 G21 G20 G19 G18 G17 G16 G15 G14 G13 G12 G11 G10 G9 G8 G7 G6 G5 G4 G3 G2 G1

Requests — F29 F28 F27 F26 F25 F24 F23 F22 F21 F20 F19 F18 F17 F16 F15 F14 F13 F12 F11 F10 F9 F8 F7 F6 F5 F4 F3 F2 F1

Vocal Imitation — E20 E19 E18 E17 E16 E15 E14 E13 E12 E11 E10 E9 E8 E7 E6 E5 E4 E3 E2 E1

Imitation — D27 D26 D25 D24 D23 D22 D21 D20 D19 D18 D17 D16 D15 D14 D13 D12 D11 D10 D9 D8 D7 D6 D5 D4 D3 D2 D1

Receptive Language — C57 C56 C55 C54 C53 C52 C51 C50 C49 C48 C47 C46 C45 C44 C43 C42 C41 C40 C39 C38 C37 C36 C35 C34 C33 C32 C31 C30 C29 C28 C27 C26 C25 C24 C23 C22 C21 C20 C19 C18 C17 C16 C15 C14 C13 C12 C11 C10 C9 C8 C7 C6 C5 C4 C3 C2 C1

Visual Performance — B27 B26 B25 B24 B23 B22 B21 B20 B19 B18 B17 B16 B15 B14 B13 B12 B11 B10 B9 B8 B7 B6 B5 B4 B3 B2 B1

Cooperation & Reinforcer Effectiveness — A19 A18 A17 A16 A15 A14 A13 A12 A11 A10 A9 A8 A7 A6 A5 A4 A3 A2 A1

Copyright © 1994-2006 By Behavior Analysts, Inc.   Please do not duplicate

Assessment of Basic Language and Learning Skills - Revised

Skill Tracking System

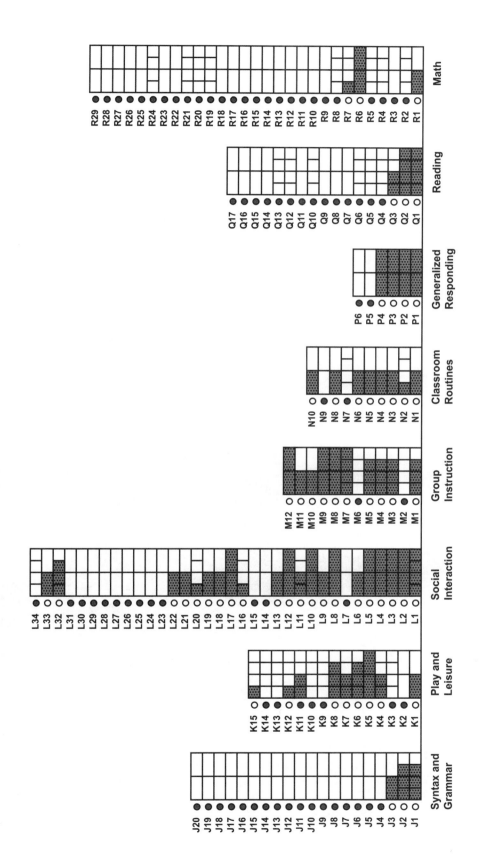

Assessment of Basic Language and Learning Skills - Revised
Skill Tracking System

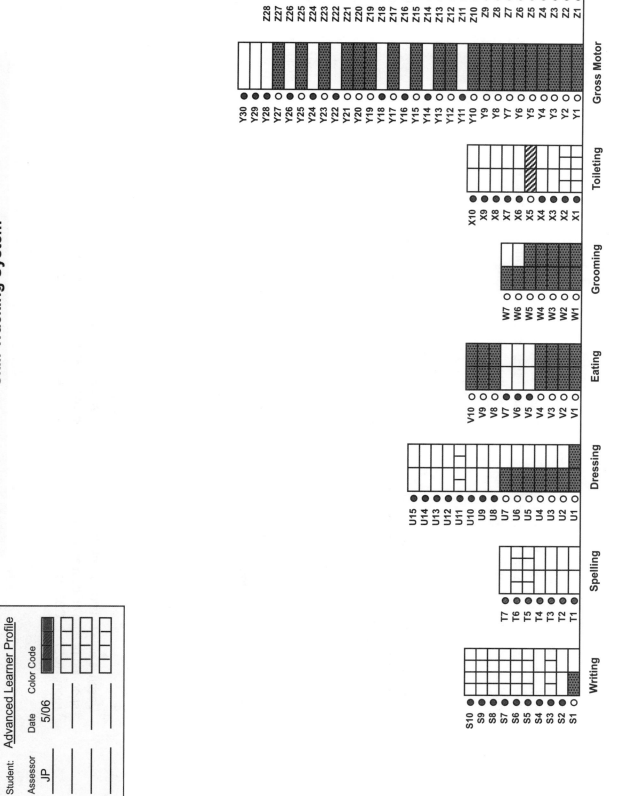

Appendix 3: Sample "Advanced Learner" IEP

CURRENT LEVEL

Jason is able to match objects and pictures to identical items (B3&5=4, B4 & 6=2), and is able to match blocks on a design card (B9=4).

Jason is able to complete inset puzzles and put together 8–piece puzzles in a frame. (B1, 10 & 11=4)

Jason is able to finish an "ABAB" and "ABCABC" pattern without prompts. (B13=4)

Jason is able to take objects to a specified person or location within a room. (C27=2, C28=4)

OBJECTIVE

Visual Performance

1 When given a model of a visual pattern, Jason will be able to make a block design that matches a picture using up to 5 blocks when given more blocks than are necessary to complete the task. (B12)

2 Jason will be able to put together a variety of 8–piece (or more) puzzles without frames. (B14 & 15)

3 When given a sample sequence pattern consisting of items, Jason will arrange additional items to extend the pattern following the original sequence. (B22)

Receptive Language Skills

4 Jason will be able to go independently to any known person and request a specified object and bring back the object. (C29 & 30)

CRITERIA

As measured by:
_____ Teacher observation
_____ Work Samples
_X_ Data Collection
_____ Speech Therapist
_80_ % Accuracy Criterion
NEW _X_ MET _____
CONTINUE_____ DELETE_____

As measured by:
_____ Teacher observation
_____ Work Samples
_X_ Data Collection
_____ Speech Therapist
_80_ % Accuracy Criterion
NEW _X_ MET _____
CONTINUE_____ DELETE_____

As measured by:
_____ Teacher observation
_____ Work Samples
_X_ Data Collection
_____ Speech Therapist
_80_ % Accuracy Criterion
NEW _X_ MET _____
CONTINUE_____ DELETE_____

As measured by:
_____ Teacher observation
_____ Work Samples
_X_ Data Collection
_____ Speech Therapist
_80_ % Accuracy Criterion
NEW _X_ MET _____
CONTINUE_____ DELETE_____

Appendix 3: Sample "Advanced Learner" IEP

CURRENT LEVEL	# OBJECTIVE	CRITERIA
Jason is able to receptively identify and to tact (label) the prepositions "on", "in", and "under". (C51=2, G35=1)	5 Jason will be able to receptively identify and tact (i.e., label) a total of at least 10 prepositions. (C51 & G35)	As measured by: ____ Teacher observation ____ Work Samples _X_ Data Collection ____ Speech Therapist _80_ % Accuracy Criterion NEW _X_ MET ____ CONTINUE____ DELETE____
Jason is able to receptively identify the pronouns "your," and "my." (C52=2, G37=0)	6 Jason will be able to receptively identify and tact (i.e., label) at least 6 pronouns. (C52 & G37)	As measured by: ____ Teacher observation ____ Work Samples _X_ Data Collection ____ Speech Therapist _80_ % Accuracy Criterion NEW _X_ MET ____ CONTINUE____ DELETE____
Jason is able to receptively identify at least 10 adjectives (i.e., "The red one"). (C24 & 48=3)	7 Jason will be able to select a specified item which has two specified characteristics (i.e., "The big red ball"). (C49)	As measured by: ____ Teacher observation ____ Work Samples _X_ Data Collection ____ Speech Therapist _80_ % Accuracy Criterion NEW _X_ MET ____ CONTINUE____ DELETE____
Jason is able to receptively identify at least 5 items when told either its function, one of its features, or given its class. (C37-39=2)	**Receptive by Function, Feature, or Class** 8 Jason will be able to select 1 item from a display of 3 items when told one of the item's functions, features, or class for 2 aspects of at least 50 of his known items (e.g., "Touch the one you eat"). (C37-39)	As measured by: ____ Teacher observation ____ Work Samples _X_ Data Collection ____ Speech Therapist _80_ % Accuracy Criterion NEW _X_ MET ____ CONTINUE____ DELETE____

Appendix 3: Sample "Advanced Learner" IEP

CURRENT LEVEL	# OBJECTIVE	CRITERIA
	Imitation	
Jason is able to imitate a wide variety of motor movements but requires at least one verbal prompt to imitate the speed of an action. (D1-5=4, D17=1)	9 Jason will imitate a gross motor activity matching the speed of a model. (D17)	As measured by: __X__ Teacher observation _____ Work Samples _____ Data Collection _____ Speech Therapist __80__ % Accuracy Criterion NEW__X__ MET_____ DELETE_____ CONTINUE_____
Jason is able complete a two sequence motor activity with at least one verbal prompt. (D20=1)	10 Jason will be able to imitate a sequence of motor activities without additional prompts (i.e., "Clap hands, then thighs, then tap fingers"). (D20)	As measured by: _____ Teacher observation _____ Work Samples __X__ Data Collection _____ Speech Therapist __80__ % Accuracy Criterion NEW__X__ MET_____ DELETE_____ CONTINUE_____
	Requesting	
Jason is able to mand for (i.e., request) a variety of items and activities. He also occasionally mands for information using "what," but does not request information using "who" or "where" questions. (F1-8= maximum scores, F19=2, F20 & 21=0)	11 Jason will be able to ask for information using "who" and "where" questions. (F20 & 21)	As measured by: _____ Teacher observation _____ Work Samples __X__ Data Collection _____ Speech Therapist __80__ % Accuracy Criterion NEW__X__ MET_____ DELETE_____ CONTINUE_____
Jason is able to mand for one item needed to complete a task (paper). (F9=1)	12 Jason will be able to mand (request) for any known item needed to complete a task. (F9)	As measured by: _____ Teacher observation _____ Work Samples __X__ Data Collection _____ Speech Therapist __80__ % Accuracy Criterion NEW__X__ MET_____ DELETE_____ CONTINUE_____

Appendix 3: Sample "Advanced Learner" IEP

CURRENT LEVEL	# OBJECTIVE	CRITERIA
	Tacts (Labeling)	
Jason is able to tact (label) over 150 items and receptively identify at least 20 pictures of actions and tact (label) at least 10 pictures of actions. (C35=4, G1-4=4, G7&8=3)	13 Jason will tact (label) 20 common actions (both on-going and pictures). (G7 & 8)	As measured by: ___ Teacher observation ___ Work Samples _X_ Data Collection ___ Speech Therapist _80_ % Accuracy Criterion NEW _X_ MET ___ CONTINUE ___ DELETE ___
Jason is able to tact (label) at least 2 items when told either its function, or one of its features. (G15 & 16=1, G17=0)	14 When given a visual display (pictures or items), Jason will be able to label at least 50 items when told their function, feature, or class. (G15-17)	As measured by: ___ Teacher observation ___ Work Samples _X_ Data Collection ___ Speech Therapist _80_ % Accuracy Criterion NEW _X_ MET ___ CONTINUE ___ DELETE ___
Jason is able to receptively identify at least 10 adjectives (i.e., "The red one") but is unable to tact using adjectives other than the color of the item. (C24=3, G13=2)	15 Jason will be able to receptively identify and tact (i.e., label) items using adjectives, for at least 15 non-color adjectives (e.g., big/little). (C24 & G13)	As measured by: ___ Teacher observation ___ Work Samples _X_ Data Collection ___ Speech Therapist _80_ % Accuracy Criterion NEW _X_ MET ___ CONTINUE ___ DELETE ___
	Intraverbals	
Jason is able to respond to at least 5 intraverbal fill-ins regarding the functions of items but is unable to fill in the features nor class of items. (H6=2, H8&9=2, H14 & H16-18=0)	16 Jason will correctly respond to 25 intraverbal fill-ins ("Barney is a ____," ""When your hair is messy, you need to ____," etc.). (H6, 8, 9, 14, 16-18))	As measured by: ___ Teacher observation ___ Work Samples _X_ Data Collection ___ Speech Therapist _80_ % Accuracy Criterion NEW _X_ MET ___ CONTINUE ___ DELETE ___

Appendix 3: Sample "Advanced Learner" IEP

CURRENT LEVEL

Jason is unable to give multiple responses to specific categories. (H15=0)

Jason is able to state his first name and age. (H5=2)

Jason does play with toys, but needs partial prompts to engage in a wider variety of responses with toys. (K7=2)

Jason does play but not with a definite theme. (K10=0)

OBJECTIVE

17 Jason will be able to verbally provide members of specific categories. (H15)

18 Jason will be able to provide answers to 4 questions regarding personal information (first and last name, age, and phone number). (H5)

Play & Leisure Skills

19 Jason will play with toys engaging in multiple responses consistent with an identifiable theme, for at least 5 activities or 5 toys. (K7)

20 Jason will participate in sociodramatic play activities in which he pretends to be at least 5 different characters (e.g., cook, doctor, action figures). (K10)

CRITERIA

As measured by:
___ Teacher observation
___ Work Samples
_X_ Data Collection
___ Speech Therapist
_80_ % Accuracy Criterion
NEW _X_ MET___
CONTINUE___ DELETE___

As measured by:
___ Teacher observation
___ Work Samples
_X_ Data Collection
___ Speech Therapist
_80_ % Accuracy Criterion
NEW _X_ MET___
CONTINUE___ DELETE___

As measured by:
___ Teacher observation
___ Work Samples
_X_ Data Collection
___ Speech Therapist
_80_ % Accuracy Criterion
NEW _X_ MET___
CONTINUE___ DELETE___

As measured by:
___ Teacher observation
___ Work Samples
_X_ Data Collection
___ Speech Therapist
_80_ % Accuracy Criterion
NEW _X_ MET___
CONTINUE___ DELETE___

Appendix 3: Sample "Advanced Learner" IEP

CURRENT LEVEL	# OBJECTIVE	CRITERIA
	Social Interaction	As measured by:
Jason initiates greetings with adults, but needs partial prompts to initiate greetings with peers. (L21=1)	21 Jason will initiate and return greetings with peers without prompting. (L10 & 21)	_____ Teacher observation _____ Work Samples __X__ Data Collection _____ Speech Therapist _80_ % Accuracy Criterion NEW _X_ MET _____ CONTINUE_____ DELETE_____
	Group Instruction	As measured by:
Jason will follow instructions that are known to him when in a group comprised of three students, but his responding decreases considerably when he is in a group comprised of four students. (M1 & 3-5=3, M2 & 6=0)	22 Jason will follow instructions that are known by him (e.g., touch known items, imitate an action, etc.) presented to a group of four students. (M1-6)	__X_ Teacher observation _____ Work Samples _____ Data Collection _____ Speech Therapist _80_ % Accuracy Criterion NEW _X_ MET _____ CONTINUE_____ DELETE_____
Jason has difficulty taking turns and answering known questions when in a group comprised of four or more students. (M10 & 11=1)	23 Jason will appropriately take turns with three other students during group instruction activities. (M10 & 11)	__X_ Teacher observation _____ Work Samples _____ Data Collection _____ Speech Therapist _80_ % Accuracy Criterion NEW _X_ MET _____ CONTINUE_____ DELETE_____
	Reading Skills	As measured by:
Jason knows the upper—case and lower—case letters of the alphabet and is able to receptively identify the sounds of several letters. (Q3=2, Q4=0)	24 Jason will be able to tact (i.e., label) the sounds of 15 letters. (Q4)	_____ Teacher observation _____ Work Samples __X__ Data Collection _____ Speech Therapist _80_ % Accuracy Criterion NEW _X_ MET _____ CONTINUE_____ DELETE_____

Appendix 3: Sample "Advanced Learner" IEP

CURRENT LEVEL	#	OBJECTIVE	CRITERIA
Jason is unable to match words to pictures of items. (Q5=0)	25	Jason will be able to match at least 10 words to their corresponding picture. (Q5)	As measured by: ___ Teacher observation ___ Work Samples _X_ Data Collection ___ Speech Therapist _80_ % Accuracy Criterion NEW _X_ MET ___ CONTINUE ___ DELETE ___
		Math	
Jason is unable to match a numeral to the same number of items. (R8=0)	26	Jason will be able to match a numeral to the same number of items given to him for at least 20 items. (R8)	As measured by: ___ Teacher observation ___ Work Samples _X_ Data Collection ___ Speech Therapist _80_ % Accuracy Criterion NEW _X_ MET ___ CONTINUE ___ DELETE ___
Jason is able to tact (i.e., label) the numerals up to 10. (R7=1)	27	Jason will be able to tact (i.e., label) the numerals 1 to 31. (R7)	As measured by: ___ Teacher observation ___ Work Samples _X_ Data Collection ___ Speech Therapist _80_ % Accuracy Criterion NEW _X_ MET ___ CONTINUE ___ DELETE ___
Jason is able to count out 3 objects from a larger set. (R5=0)	28	Jason will be able to count out objects from a larger set for up to 20 objects. (R5)	As measured by: ___ Teacher observation ___ Work Samples _X_ Data Collection ___ Speech Therapist _80_ % Accuracy Criterion NEW _X_ MET ___ CONTINUE ___ DELETE ___

Appendix 3: Sample "Advanced Learner" IEP

CURRENT LEVEL

Jason is able to rote count to the number 8. (R1=1 & R2=0)

Jason can trace, but does not accurately stay on the lines. (S3=0)

Jason needs physical prompts to color within a defined area. (S2=0)

Jason is able to ask to have his diaper changed when needed. (X1=0)

OBJECTIVE

29 Jason will be able to rote count without prompts to the number 20. (R2)

Writing Skills

30 Jason will be able to trace simple straight and curved lines, and shapes staying within 1/4 inch of the model. (S3)

31 Jason will be able to color within lined areas without prompts. (S2 & Z10)

Self-Help Skills

32 Jason will urinate in the toilet at least 2 times a day. (X1)

CRITERIA

As measured by:
_____ Teacher observation
_____ Work Samples
__X_ Data Collection
_____ Speech Therapist
_80_ % Accuracy Criterion
NEW _X_ MET _____
CONTINUE_____ DELETE_____

As measured by:
_____ Teacher observation
__X_ Work Samples
_____ Data Collection
_____ Speech Therapist
_80_ % Accuracy Criterion
NEW _X_ MET _____
CONTINUE_____ DELETE_____

As measured by:
_____ Teacher observation
__X_ Work Samples
_____ Data Collection
_____ Speech Therapist
_80_ % Accuracy Criterion
NEW _X_ MET _____
CONTINUE_____ DELETE_____

As measured by:
_____ Teacher observation
_____ Work Samples
__X_ Data Collection
_____ Speech Therapist
_80_ % Accuracy Criterion
NEW _X_ MET _____
CONTINUE_____ DELETE_____

Appendix 3: Sample "Advanced Learner" IEP

CURRENT LEVEL

OBJECTIVE

CRITERIA

Fine Motor

33 Jason will be able to cut out simple shapes staying within 1/4 inch of the line. (Z16 & 27)

Jason can cut with scissors, but does not accurately cut on the line. (Z16=0)

As measured by:
___ Teacher observation
_X_ Work Samples
___ Data Collection
___ Speech Therapist
_80_ % Accuracy Criterion
NEW _X_ MET ___
CONTINUE___ DELETE___

Behavior Plan

34 Jason will reduce instances of hitting staff and throwing materials to 50% of baseline levels.

Jason hits and/or throws materials approximately 4 out of 13 sessions a day. (A17=2)

As measured by:
___ Teacher observation
___ Work Samples
_X_ Data Collection
___ Speech Therapist
___ % Accuracy Criterion
NEW _X_ MET___
CONTINUE___ DELETE___

References

Cooper, J. O., Heron, T. E., & Heward, W. L. (1987). *Applied Behavior Analysis.* Englewood Cliffs, NJ: Prentice-Hall, Inc.

Foxx, R. M. (1982). *Decreasing behaviors of severely retarded and autistic persons.* Champaign, IL: Research Press.

Foxx, R. M. (1982). *Increasing behaviors of severely retarded and autistic persons.* Champaign, IL: Research Press.

Lerman, D. C., Parten, M., Addison, L. R., Vorndran, C. M., Volkert, V. M., & Kodak, T. (2005). A methodology for assessing the functions of emerging speech in children with developmental disabilities. *Journal of Applied Behavior Analysis, 38,* 303-316.

Martin, G. & Pear, J. (2002). *Behavior modification: What it is and how to do it (7th Edition).* Englewood Cliffs, NJ: Prentice-Hall, Inc.

Palmer, D. C. (1998). The speaker as listener: The interpretation of structural regularities in verbal behavior. *The Analysis of Verbal Behavior,* 15, 3-16.

Palmer, D. C. (1996). Achieving parity: The role of automatic reinforcement. *Journal of the Experimental Analysis of Behavior,* 65, 289-290.

Partington, J. W., Dwiggins, G., & Osnes, P. (in preparation). *An analysis of the performance of young typically developing children on The Assessment of Basic Language and learning Skills.*

Partington, J. W., & Sundberg, M. L. (1998). *The assessment of basic language and learning skills.* Danville, CA: Behavior Analysts, Inc.

Payne, S., Radicchi, J., Rosellini, L., Deutchman, L., & Darch, C. (1983). *Structuring classrooms for academic success.* Eugene, OR: Association for Direct Instruction.

Ross, D. E., & Greer, R. D. (2003). Generalized imitation and the mand: Inducing first instances of speech in young children with autism. *Research in Developmental Disabilities*, 24, 58-74.

Skinner, B. F. (1957). *Verbal behavior.* New York: Appleton-Century-Crofts.

Sloane, H. N., & MacAuley, B. D. (Eds.) (1968). *Operant procedures in remedial speech and language training.* Boston: Houghton Mifflin.

Spradlin, J. E. (1963). Assessment of speech and language of retarded children: The Parsons language sample. *Journal of Speech and Hearing Disorders Monograph*, 10, 8-31.

Sundberg, M. L. (1983). Language. In J. L. Matson, & S. E. Breuning (Eds.), *Assessing the mentally retarded* (pp. 285-310). New York: Grune & Stratton.

Sundberg, M. L., & Michael, J. (1998). *A collection of reprints on verbal behavior.* Danville, CA: Behavior Analysts, Inc.

Sundberg, M. L., & Partington, J. W. (1998). *Teaching Language to Children with Autism or Other Developmental Disabilities.* Danville, CA: Behavior Analysts, Inc.

Sundberg, M. L., Ray, D. A., Braam, S. J., Stafford, M. W., Rueber, T., & Braam, C. (1979). The use of B.F. Skinner's Analysis of Verbal Behavior for Language Assessment and Training. *Western Michigan University Behavioral Monograph #8.* Kalamazoo, MI: Western Michigan University

Wynn, J. W., & Smith, T., (2003). Generalization between receptive and expressive language in young children with autism. *Behavioral Interventions*, *18*, 245-266.